STOICISM
TODAY

Selected Writings

Volume One

Edited by
Patrick Ussher

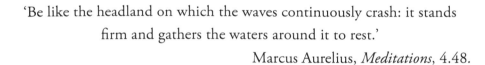

'Be like the headland on which the waves continuously crash: it stands firm and gathers the waters around it to rest.'

Marcus Aurelius, *Meditations*, 4.48.

ABOUT STOICISM TODAY

The *Stoicism Today* team is comprised of academics, based at The University of Exeter, King's College, University of London and Queen Mary, University of London, and psychotherapists, based in the U.K. and Canada, working together to create Stoic resources for the modern day. It has organized two international 'Stoic Weeks' (November 2012, 2013). Around 2,200 people took part in Stoic Week 2013. They were given a 38-page booklet to follow with day-by-day exercises and advice, and there was a public day in London attended by over 200 people. The week was featured in several publications, including *The Toronto Globe & Mail*, *The Daily Telegraph*, *Channel 4 Online*, and *The Spectator*. It was also featured on radio, including BBC Radio 4, BBC Wales and the BBC World Service. There is also a 'Stoicism Today' blog (see link below), from which the pieces in this first volume have been selected. It has had almost 400,000 hits in its first 18 months. There will be a Stoic Week 2014, from the 24th to 30th of November, and a London event at Queen Mary, University of London, on November 29th.

Jules Evans, Gabriele Galluzzo, Gill Garratt, Christopher Gill, Tim LeBon Donald Robertson, John Sellars, and Patrick Ussher are the members of the *Stoicism Today* team.

By purchasing this book, you are contributing to a fund to support *Stoicism Today* projects.

Internet References:
Blog: http://blogs.exeter.ac.uk/stoicismtoday/
Youtube Channel: https://www.youtube.com/user/StoicismToday
Twitter: https://twitter.com/StoicWeek
Facebook Group: https://www.facebook.com/groups/Stoicism/

TABLE OF CONTENTS

CONTRIBUTORS

Corey Anton (Ph.D., Purdue University, 1998) is Professor of Communication Studies at Grand Valley State University. His books include *Selfhood and Authenticity* (SUNY Press, 2001) and *Sources of Significance: Worldly Rejuvenation and Neo-Stoic Heroism* (Duquesne University Press, 2010).

Jan-Fredrik Braseth is a Norwegian philosopher with an MA in philosophy and an education as a philosophical counsellor. He lives in Oslo and works as a counsellor for people who are unemployed because of ill-health. His website is: www.janfredrik.no.

Paul Bryson is a lawyer living and working in the Greater Columbus Metropolitan Area, Ohio. He has been interested in Stoic philosophy since encountering the works of Seneca as a high school Latin student. He blogs at: stoiclawyer.wordpress.com.

Michael Burton is a Canadian Secondary School teacher working in the United Kingdom. He first encountered Stoicism as a secondary school philosophy student and has been inspired by Stoic thinking ever since. He blogs about matters surrounding both philosophy and education at: burtonsblogs12.blogspot.co.uk/.

Ben Butina works in the field of training and development. He has an MA in Counseling and is currently pursuing his PhD in Psychology. In addition to Stoicism, He has an interest in Eastern philosophy and religion. He lives with his wife and children in Latrobe, Pennslyvania. He blogs at: approximatelyforever.com.

Bob Collopy is an author, pilot, marketing director/branch manager for a real estate brokerage, and a partner in a new start-up company, funded by Arizona State University, which is aimed at creating and selling a new type of dive computer for scuba divers. He is also an Eagle Scout.

Stephen J. Costello is the founder and director of the Viktor Frankl Institute of Ireland. He is a philosopher, logotherapist/existential analyst and author. He has been lecturing in philosophy and psychology for over twenty years in University College Dublin, Trinity College Dublin and, more recently, in the Dublin Business School. He is the author of *The Irish Soul: In Dialogue* (The Liffey Press, 2002), *The Pale Criminal: Psychoanalytic Perspectives* (Karnac Books, 2002), *18 Reasons Why Mothers Hate Their Babies: A Philosophy of Childhood* (Eloquent Books, 2009), *Hermeneutics and the Psychoanalysis of Religion* (Peter Lang AG., 2009), *The Ethics of Happiness: An Existential Analysis* (Wyndham Hall Press, 2011), *What are Friends For?: Insights from the Great Philosophers* (Raider Publishing International, 2011), *Philosophy and the Flow of Presence* (Cambridge Scholars Publishing, 2013), and *The Truth about Lying* (The Liffey Press, 2013).

Kelly Coyne is co-author, with her husband, Erik Knutzen, of *The Urban Homestead: Your Guide to Self-Sufficient Living in the Heart of the City* (Process, 2010) and *Making It: Radical Home Ec for a Post Consumer World* (Rodale Press, 2011). Her website is: www.rootsimple.com.

James Davinport is a pseudonym. He lives and works in London.

Michel Daw has been a teacher of adults for over 20 years. He is an author, speaker and blogger on all things Stoic. Michel runs, with his wife, Pamela Daw, a series of Stoic Workshops in his local community, which meets regularly, in Canada. He blogs at livingthestoiclife.org.

Pamela Daw is mother of three adult children, and has been married to Michel Daw for 28 years. With her husband, she runs a Stoic community, which meets regularly, in Canada. She blogs at: musingsofastoicwoman. blogspot.com.

Jules Evans *is author of Philosophy for Life and Other Dangerous Situations* (Rider, 2013). He is policy director for the Centre of the History of Emotions at Queen Mary College, University of London. More recently, he has developed and run a course of practical philosophy for Low Moss Prison in Scotland and Saracens rugby club in the UK. His website is: philosophyforlife.org.

Jen Farren is a freelance writer living in the Balkans. She writes about Balkan Art, Culture and Ideas, past and present, and blogs about this at: gotirana.wordpress.com. Her career is in research, analysis, writing and communications for London Underground, Police and Government. She has written for IROKO Theatre, Royal Docks Project and Heritage Lottery Fund.

Mark Garvey is the author of *Stylized (Touchstone, 2009), Come Together (Thomson, 2006), and Searching for Mary (Plume, 1998). His* articles and essays have appeared in *The Wall Street Journal, The Oxford American, Writer's Digest*, and elsewhere. He lives in Cincinnati, Ohio, and blogs at OldAnswers.com.

Christopher Gill is Emeritus Professor of Ancient Thought at the University of Exeter, U.K. He has written extensively on ancient philosophy. His books include *The Structured Self in Hellenistic and Roman Thought* (Oxford University Press, 2006), *Naturalistic Psychology in Galen & Stoicism* (Oxford University Press, 2010). He has also written the introduction and notes for *Epictetus: Discourses, Fragments, Handbook* and *Marcus Aurelius: Meditations*, both part of the Oxford World's Classics series.

Ryan Holiday is a media strategist and prominent writer on strategy and business. He served as director of marketing at American Apparel for many years. His books include *Trust Me I'm Lying: Confessions of a Media Manipulator* (Portfolio, 2010) and, on Stoicism, *The Obstacle is the Way: The Timeless Art of Turning Trials into Triumph* (Portfolio, 2013). His website is: RyanHoliday.net.

Laura Inman is an independent scholar, free-lance writer, tutor, and retired attorney. Her work as a Brontë scholar includes *The Poetic World of Emily Brontë* (Sussex Academic Press, 2014) and articles on Emily Brontë in *Brontë Studies* and *Victorians: Journal of Culture and Literature*. Her essays on literature and Stoicism and short stories have appeared in on-line magazines and blogs, including her own blog, thelivingphilosopher.com, a Stoic and literary guide to living. She holds a J.D. from The Law School of the University of Texas at Austin, a B.A. in French from the University of Arizona, and a Masters in English Education from Manhattanville College in Purchase, New York.

Kevin Kennedy is a German-American historian, writer, and tour-guide living and working in Potsdam, Germany. He specializes in the early modern history of Prussia, Germany, and Central Europe, but is also interested in urban studies, philosophy, and, of course, Stoicism.

Erik Knutzen is the co-author, with his wife Kelly Coyne, of *The Urban Homestead: Your Guide to Self-Sufficient Living in the Heart of the City* (Process, 2010) and *Making It: Radical Home Ec for a Post Consumer World* (Rodale Press, 2011). His website is rootsimple.com.

Tim LeBon is a UKCP (UK Council for Psychotherapy) registered therapist and works in the NHS in IAPT (the *Improving Access to Psychological Therapies* scheme) using Cognitive Behavioural Therapy which he combines with a private practice as a counsellor and life coach in Central London. He is the founding editor of the journal *Practical Philosophy* and author of *Wise Therapy* (Sage, 2001) and *Achieve Your Potential with Positive Psychology* (Hodder, 2014). His website is www.timlebon.com.

Chris Lowe lives in Halifax, Nova Scotia. His interest in Stoicism started in late 2013. He studies the classic works of Epictetus and Marcus Aurelius, whilst also maintaining an interest in similarly based Eastern philosophies. Chris is a self-directed student of Stoicism and blogs at stoicism.ca.

Antonia Macaro has a background as a UKCP-registered existential psychotherapist and counsellor in the drugs and alcohol field. She has an MA in philosophy and has been involved in the philosophical counselling movement since its early days in the UK. She has written *Reason, Virtue and Psychotherapy* (Wiley-Blackwell, 2006) and, with Julian Baggini, *The Shrink and the Sage* (Icon Books, 2012). In November 2013, she took part in the roundtable discussion at the Stoicism for Everyday Life day in London. Her website is: antoniamacaro.com.

Aditya Nain holds an MA in Philosophy from the University of Pune, India, and a Diploma in Finance from the University of London. While being an Assistant Professor at SSLA (Symbiosis School for Liberal Arts) in Pune, he is also pursuing his PhD studies at the Indian Institute of Technology, Bombay (IITB) under the program for "College Teachers", in the area of the Philosophy of Money. He blogs at: adityanain.com.

Tim Rayner is Co-Founder and Director of One Million Acts of Innovation (Australia). He has taught philosophy at the University of Sydney and the University of New South Wales, Australia. He is the author of the transformation manual *Life Changing: A Philosophical Guide* (2012) and the award-winning short film, 'Coalition of the Willing' (2010). His website is: timrayner.net.

Donald Robertson is a cognitive-behavioural psychotherapist, trainer, and author who specialises in the treatment of anxiety and the use of CBT and clinical hypnotherapy. He is author of *Teach Yourself Stoicism and the Art of Happiness* (Teach Yourself, 2013), *Resilience: Teach Yourself How to Survive and Thrive in Any Situation* (Teach Yourself, 2012) and *The Philosophy of Cognitive Behavioral Therapy: Stoic Philosophy as Rational and Cognitive Psychotherapy* (Karnac Books, 2010). He blogs at: philosophy-of-cbt.com.

Helen Rudd suffered a traumatic brain injury in 2006, after which she was in a coma for 3 weeks. Later, she was severely depressed when she realised how much her life had changed, mainly because she was no longer able-bodied. Through Stoicism, however, her life has opened up and she now makes the most of every day.

Roberto Sans-Boza graduated from Cadiz University in Spain in 1991. He completed his clinical neurophysiology specialist training in San Carlos University Hospital, Madrid and additional subspecialist training in electrocorticography and videotelemetry at the Montreal Neurological Institute (Canada). Dr Sans-Boza got his first Consultant post in 1998 in The Walton Centre, Liverpool and Glan Clwyd Hospital, North Wales. He joined the Clinical Neurophysiology department in Derriford in 2013.

John Sellars is a Research Fellow at King's College, University of London. He has written two books on Stoic philosophy: *Stoicism (Routledge, 2006) and The Art of Living: The Stoics on the Nature and Function of Philosophy (Bloomsbury Academic, 2013)*. His website is: www.johnsellars.org.uk.

Jeff Traylor has a wealth of corrections experience, ranging from implementing the furlough program at the maximum security Ohio Penitentiary to serving as the cognitive skills instructor at a community based correctional facility. He has served on the faculty of the Michigan Judicial Institute and has trained hundreds of professionals ranging from parole officers to social workers. He earned his graduate degree from The Ohio State University and is the author of a series of Ohio travel books called *Life in the Slow Lane* (King of the Road Press).

Patrick Ussher is a PhD student at the University of Exeter, working on Stoic ethical development. His MA dissertation compared Stoicism and 'Western' Buddhism. He edits and manages the *Stoicism Today* blog.

Matt Van Natta is a practicing Stoic who blogs at: immoderatestoic. com. He is also a husband, a father, and an emergency management professional. Stoicism serves him well in each of those roles.

FOREWORD

Stephen J. Costello, Ph.D.

This book reflects and represents a wide-ranging cornucopia of topics and themes, from Stoic ethics and emotions to fatherhood, feelings and Viktor Frankl, from Stoic mayors and mindfulness to practical philosophy, parenting, psychotherapy and prisons, from Star Trek and Socrates to Stoic lawyers, literature and living in general. As such, there is something in this eclectic compilation for everyone.

There are two signifiers in the title of this edited edition: 'Stoicism' and 'today'. That suggests that ancient Athenian Stoicism – that school of Hellenistic practical philosophy – has something still to say to us today, in our times. The Stoics struggled with suffering; they wanted to conform their will to the world; they wished to cultivate virtue in order to flourish. They believed that a person's behaviour was more important than his words. They viewed philosophy less as an arcane, academic, theoretical and difficult discipline and more as a way of life for those who were in love with Wisdom (*sophia*) and the Good (*agathon*).

From its very inception, the philosophy proved popular. That's because it was practical as well as profound. It even found favour with an Emperor – Marcus Aurelius – who himself became a Stoic and penned the famous *Meditations*. However, another Emperor – Justinian I – closed down these 'pagan' schools of philosophy in 529 AD, because they were perceived to be incompatible with Constantinian Christianity (Constantine the Great had called the first Council of Nicea in 325 AD). However, Stoic ideas permeated the spirituality of St. Ignatius of Loyola, to name but one religious founder, who christianised earlier Stoic spiritual exercises, as many others would.

So what's the big attraction? Stoics want us to practise fortitude in the face of blows of fate; they want us to develop self-control especially over destructive and negative emotions; they want us to improve our moral and spiritual wellbeing; they want us to align our lives with the divine *logos* permeating all of creation. They want us to be passionately and joyfully peaceful, as well as wise, courageous, disciplined and just. They want us to examine our lives and practise daily disciplines – spiritual exercises – which will become habits of the heart to help us here and now. They want us to be indifferent to indifferent things and to concentrate on what we can control and what we can choose, and to let go of the things we can't. They want us to love in harmony and be in a state of happiness, to help each other and live in love. Because we are disturbed not by things but by the interpretations our minds put on things, by the views we take of things. And aren't these ideals worth pursuing, worth having, worth being? In short, they want us to live more meaningfully and less mindlessly.

Founded by Zeno, Stoicism attracted into its ranks men of the stature of Seneca the lawyer, Epictetus the former slave and Marcus Aurelius the Emperor. They stand out as stars of the first nova. Their writings, be they Seneca's *Letters*, Epictetus's *Discourses*, or Marcus Aurelius's *Meditations*, inspire, uplift, ennoble. They persuade and gently chide even as they encourage. In the end, nothing can really touch the soul, our inner citadel. Much is within our power and province. And the rest? The rest belongs to God. It is His business not ours. The point is not how long we live but how nobly: life is about depth not duration. And this too the ancient, noble Stoa taught. Don't you want to be free? Stop being a slave therefore. The Stoics have shown us all a way and shone their lanterns to illuminate the darkness of our times. It is up to us to follow them. Or not, as the case may be.

Dublin, July 2014.

INTRODUCTION

As a robust philosophy and way of life, with the key claim that the cultivation of virtue can lead both to meeting life's challenges successfully and also to leading a structured, purposeful life which contributes to the common good, it is easy to see why interest in Stoicism has been on the rise. For, as long as the question "How can I live well?" is raised, Stoicism will always be happy to provide its answers.

Many of these answers are presented in this volume, as worked out by those who follow, or have made use of, the Stoic path today. Taken as a whole, the Stoic theory, advice and life stories within are at the heart of this book (Parts I, III, IV). You'll read powerful examples of living a Stoic life, from facing adversity (and turning it on its head), to basing one's profession on Stoic ethics and values, to conquering the fear of death as well as reflections on the nature of happiness itself. Throughout, it becomes clear that Stoicism has no qualms about being a *realistic* philosophy - it does not shy away from the difficult realities of life - but also, starting from this basis, it provides answers to how to live in the face of these very difficulties. In a culture where 'feeling good' is often the norm to be pursued (not something, *de facto*, that is so easy when times are tough), the idea of pursuing a conception of the 'good', or having an excellent state of character, that can meet these difficulties 'head on' stands out, as does the idea of structuring one's life *as a whole* around a coherent set of values.

Also included are reflections on Stoic parenting and teaching (Part V).

For the ancient Stoics, one of the principal aims in life was to fulfill your 'naturally acquired' relationships as well as possible, especially one's duties as a parent. This relationship, at the heart of Stoic cosmopolitan theory, is thoughtfully explored by a trio of Stoic fathers. Stoics did not just try to excel in their 'naturally' acquired roles however, but also in the roles they had in society. In the same spirit, what Stoicism has to offer in the classroom is also considered in Part V.

Thinking about Stoicism and its applications in the modern world is not always straightforward, and some of the issues that this presents are discussed in Part II. Does 'adapting' Stoicism run the risk of creating a 'Stoicism-Lite', a system which focusses just on techniques rather than on ethics and values? In the process of adaptation, which aspects of the ancient philosophy should be kept, which dropped and why? Or does Stoicism need to be 'adapted' at all - is it fine just the way it is? There are no definitive answers to these questions, nor should there be, but they certainly need to be asked. Any philosophical (or religious, for that matter) tradition is often in dialogue with itself and, indeed, this may be a necessary condition of putting that philosophy into practice well.

When speaking of 'adaptations', it is hard not also to think of the 'adaptation' in recent decades of certain Buddhist practices into the Western mainstream, in the form of 'mindfulness meditation', or the ability to keep one's attention focussed on the present moment. Indeed, many of those who come across Stoicism have also practised mindfulness meditation, or some form of Buddhism, and are often struck by the similarities between the two philosophies. A lot more needs to be done on working out these similarities, and more on the differences between the two systems (which I think are quite substantial), but, to get things started, three pieces that explore 'mindfulness' from Stoic and Buddhist perspectives are included in Part VII. They all take quite different approaches. The first makes the case for how mindfulness meditation can aid or inform Stoic practice whilst the second argues that there is an inherent dichotomy between Stoicism and Buddhism such that practising the 'mindfulness' of one system cannot work with the other's. And the third piece, in contrast, tries to probe whether, in classical Stoicism itself, there was something akin to what we call 'mindfulness' today.

An often-cited way in which the modern world is indebted to Stoicism has been the influence of Stoic ideas on modern psychotherapy, in particular on CBT (Cognitive Behavioural Therapy) and REBT (Rational Emotive Behavioural Therapy). Epictetus's saying that 'People are not disturbed by events but by their opinions about events' (*Handbook*, §5) was particularly influential, as were many other similarities, brought out recently by Donald Robertson (see *The Philosophy of Cognitive-Behavioural Therapy*, 2010). In Part VI, there is a reflection which considers how both CBT and Stoicism, taken together, can help in returning to good mental health. But there are also some less explored areas of similarity between Stoicism and other psychotherapeutic approaches. For example, one piece explores the work that has been done, in the light of similar work in the field of 'Positive Psychology', a branch of psychology concerned with values, strengths and finding meaning, to measure scientifically how effective Stoicism actually is in helping people. Another piece considers Logotherapy, a therapy developed by Viktor Frankl, who survived the concentration camps of the Holocaust. Whilst the link between CBT, for example, and Stoicism is especially clear in the practice of 'challenging impressions' (or 'thoughts'), and having more balanced, accurate thinking, the similarities between Stoicism and Logotherapy run at a deeper, more philosophical level, in particular as regards the aim of seeking meaning, no matter what the circumstances. In that sense, it is not a surprise that a philosophy which claimed you could still live nobly even whilst being 'tortured on the rack' should be so similar to a philosophical therapy founded by a survivor of the Holocaust.

The last part of the book offers something a bit different, in that it explores manifestations of Stoicism in modern culture. There you will read about how Saracens rugby club in England has used Stoicism (with the aim of playing well and ethically, not just of winning), how Epictetus has helped prison inmates get their lives back together, and how Stoicism can pop up in some unlikely places, including a Sci-Fi novel and, *Star Trek*. But try, if you can, not to turn into Spock.

Two editorial points. Firstly, given the nature of a work which features so many personal opinion pieces, the interpretation of Stoicism presented throughout is not uniform. This is partly the nature of the subject, and it is likewise true of academic circles: the key, central points of Stoic ethics, for example, are still the source of much debate. Even the Stoics themselves had their own internal points of disagreement. Secondly, most of the translations of Epictetus, Marcus Aurelius and Seneca in this book come from the Loeb translations by W.A. Oldfather, C.R. Haines and R.M. Gummere respectively. In a few instances, the English has been slightly changed, so as to be more appropriate for a modern audience. Where more recent translations have been used, care has been taken to ensure that they are attributed correctly.

Finally, I would like to thank wholeheartedly all who have contributed to this volume which, it is hoped, is the first of what will become a series. Readers who would like to write about their own experience of Stoicism are encouraged to get in touch via the *Stoicism Today* website.

I hope that this collection of articles will be equally interesting to academics of Stoicism, interested in its modern applications, as well as to those who make use of Stoicism in their own lives.

Patrick Ussher
Exeter, September 2014.

STOICISM 101

John Sellars

Stoicism was one of the four principal schools of philosophy in ancient Athens, alongside Plato's Academy, Aristotle's Lyceum, and Epicurus's Garden, where it flourished for some 250 years. It proved especially popular among the Romans, attracting admirers as diverse as the statesman Seneca, the ex-slave Epictetus, and the Emperor Marcus Aurelius. The works of these three authors have come down to us and have won admirers from the Renaissance through to the present day. Although the philosophy of Stoicism as a whole is complex, embracing everything from metaphysics to astronomy to grammar, the works of the three great Roman Stoics focus on practical advice and guidance for those trying to achieve wellbeing or happiness. If you are new to Stoicism, here are four central ideas to help you get started:

Value: the only thing that is truly good is an excellent mental state, identified with virtue and reason. This is the only thing that can guarantee our happiness. External things such as money, success, fame and the like can never bring us happiness. Although there is nothing wrong with these things and they do hold value and may well form part of a good life, often the pursuit of these things actually damages the only thing that can bring us happiness: an excellent, rational mental state.

Emotions: our emotions are the project of our judgements, of thinking that something good or bad is happening or is about to happen. Many of our negative emotions are based on mistaken judgements, but because they are due to our judgements it means they are within our control. Change the judgements and you change the emotions. Despite the popular image, the Stoic does not repress or deny his emotions; instead he simply aims not to have negative emotions in the first place. The aim, therefore, is to overcome harmful, negative emotions that are based on mistaken judgments while embracing correct positive emotions, replacing anger with joy.

Nature: the Stoics suggest we ought to live in harmony with Nature. Part of what they mean by this is that we ought to acknowledge that we are but small parts of a larger, organic whole, shaped by larger processes that are ultimately out of our control. There is nothing to be gained from trying to resist these larger processes except anger, frustration, and disappointment. While there are many things in the world that we can change, there are many others we cannot and we need to understand this and accept it.

Control: in the light of what we have seen, there are some things we have control over (our judgements, our own mental state) and some things that we do not (external processes and objects). Much of our unhappiness is caused by confusing these two categories: thinking we have control over something that ultimately we do not. Happily the one thing we do have control over is the only thing that can guarantee a good, happy life.

PART ONE: STOIC THEORY

CORE IDEAS OF STOIC ETHICS IN MARCUS AURELIUS

Christopher Gill

A positive reason for seeing Stoicism as influential on Marcus is that most of the *Meditations* are strongly reminiscent of Stoic ideas, even if Marcus does not use technical Stoic vocabulary and sometimes recasts these ideas in his own distinctive ways. We can identify at least five features which were seen in this period as distinctive of Stoicism; and they match strongly marked themes in the *Meditations*. One is the idea that the virtuous life is identical with the happy life (that virtue is all that is needed to ensure happiness). Other things widely regarded as good, such as health or material prosperity and even the well-being of one's family and friends, are seen as being irrelevant for happiness; they are 'matters of indifference', even if they are naturally 'preferable'. A second theme is that emotions and desires depend directly on beliefs about what is valuable or desirable; they do not form a separate (non-rational) dimension of psychological life. The emotions and desires most people form are seen as shaped by mistaken ethical beliefs and in this sense as being psychological 'sicknesses'. A third theme is that human beings have an in-built natural inclination to benefit others. This inclination, if properly developed, is expressed both in full-hearted engagement with family and communal roles and in a readiness to accept all human beings, as such, as part of a 'brotherhood' or 'cosmic city' and as proper objects of ethical concern. These three ideas add up to a highly idealised view of human ethics and psychology, one that ancient critics thought was *over*-idealistic and unrealistic. None the less, the Stoics maintained that all human beings are fundamentally capable of progressing towards the ideal state of complete virtue and happiness, though they admitted that no one had perhaps achieved this completely. Hence, ethical life, for Stoicism, consisted in an ongoing process or journey towards this goal, a journey for which their methods of practical ethics were a means of support.

The three themes, together with the related ideas about ethical development or progress, fall within the sphere of 'ethics', as understood in Stoicism. Another distinctive theme falls within 'physics' (the study of nature) and the interface between ethics and physics. A topic of major debate at this time was whether the natural universe embodied in-built purpose or meaning or whether it was simply the random outcome of natural laws or processes. The Stoics, following Plato and Aristotle, adopted the first view, the Epicureans maintained the second, which was linked with their theory about the atomic nature of matter. The Stoic belief in in-built purpose was connected with their view that all events are determined, and that the whole sequence of events embodies divine purpose or providentiality. As this point illustrates, the Stoics saw the branches of philosophy (in this case, ethics and physics) as interconnected and mutually supporting. Thus, their belief in divine providence belonged to the study of theology (which for them formed part of physics). But this belief also helped to provide a meaningful framework for ethics; while ethics in turn made sense of ideas (such as 'good') which underpinned the notion of providentiality and thus supported the principles of theology. As this point indicates, the Stoics saw philosophy as forming a highly unified and systematic body of knowledge. The ability to trace and understand connections between different ideas and between the branches of philosophy thus formed an important part of the study of Stoicism.

An Illustrative Reading: *Meditations* **3.11**

The relevance of these ideas to the *Meditations* can be brought out in two, complementary ways. One is by examining in some depth a single passage, which shows how Marcus draws on these ideas and also how he weaves them together into a connected sequence. The other is by discussing in more general terms certain recurrent – and sometimes striking and distinctive – ways in which he treats each of these themes. First, let us look closely at this passage (3.11):

'To the preceding pieces of advice, one more should be added: always make a sketch or plan of whatever presents itself to your mind, so as to see what sort of thing it is when stripped down to its essence, as a whole and in its separate parts; and tell yourself its proper name, and the names of the elements from which it has been put together and into which it will finally be resolved. For nothing is as effective in creating greatness of mind as being able to examine methodically and truthfully everything that presents itself in life, and always viewing things in such a way as to consider what kind of use each thing serves in what kind of a universe, and what value it has to human beings as citizens of that highest of cities of which all other cities are, as it were, mere households, and what this object is that presently makes an impression on me, and what it is composed of, and how long it will naturally persist, and what virtue is needed in the face of it, such as gentleness, courage, truthfulness, good faith, simplicity, self-sufficiency, and so forth. So, as each case presents itself, you should say: this has come from god, this from the co-ordination and interweaving of the threads of fate and similar kinds of coincidence and chance, this from one of my own kind, a relation and companion, who is however ignorant of what is natural for him. But I am not ignorant of that, and thus I will therefore treat him kindly and justly, according to the natural law of companionship, though aiming at the same time at what he deserves with regard to things that are morally indifferent.'

This passage offers a clear illustration of one of Marcus's most characteristic methods of practical ethics: that is, making a 'sketch' or 'outline' of things, and 'stripping them naked' to their essential reality or core. Although this may seem at first to be a purely scientific or analytic procedure, what Marcus has in mind is getting to the *ethical* core of the situation (although, as becomes clear, this is also linked with understanding the natural world better). The 'stripping' method assumes the first of the key Stoic themes noted earlier: that our happiness depends solely on responding virtuously to situations and not at all on acquiring material or social advantages. Hence, what the method brings out is what virtues we should aim to express in that context ('what virtue is needed ... such as gentleness, courage, truthfulness, good faith, simplicity, self-sufficiency'). The passage also alludes at the end to the characteristic Stoic idea that things other than virtue, such as material wealth, are 'morally indifferent' and do not affect our happiness. Acting virtuously involves benefiting other human beings; and the passage also refers to the third theme, the idea that we should work towards regarding other human beings (in principle, all human beings) as 'brothers' and 'fellow-citizens' in a world-wide ethical community. Also, running through the passage is the fourth theme, the linkage seen by Stoics between ethics and the natural universe. Marcus reminds himself that the universe is permeated by divine providence, which shapes the way events unfold: 'as each case presents itself, you should say: this has come from god, this from the co-ordination and interweaving of the threads of fate'. In a more general way, the whole passage implies that the 'stripping' method illuminates the underlying connection between the ethical order (how we should behave) and the natural or cosmic order. Fifthly, this passage, like many others in the *Meditations*, shows the importance of underlining the connections between different, but related, themes in Stoic thought, which was famous for its 'joined-up', systematic character. Bringing out the links between ethics and physics, as the passage does, represents one aspect of this larger process.

This extract is reproduced here from pp. xv-xviii 'Introduction' by Chris-

topher Gill from "Meditations: with selected correspondence Marcus Aurelius" edited by Hard, Robin & Gill, Christopher (2011) by permission of Oxford University Press with free permission in association with author, Christopher Gill.

THE STOICS ON THE COMMUNITY OF HUMANKIND

Patrick Ussher

For our own highly individualistic society, or at least highly individu-alistic society relative to most other societies in history, in which there has been a gradual lessening of duties and obligations to one another, the idea that happiness depends on bringing to fruition the human being's inher-ently *social* nature might seem unusual. In fact, even the idea that we *are* inherently social in the first place might seem unusual. Even when we talk nowadays of benefitting oneself or other people, we think of this in terms of 'egoism' or 'altruism', as if the latter entailed 'putting our own needs aside for a moment, to think of someone else for a bit.' 'Egoism' and 'altruism' would not fit the Stoic worldview however: for them, the human being was *fundamentally* social in nature, and what was good for that human being was to be social. Such a way of regarding what is good for a human being is one reason why Stoicism can provide a helpful antidote to our own modes of thinking today, whether or not we ultimately agree with their premise.

In this article, I aim to set out what it meant, for the Stoics, to be a fundamentally social being. From our own more modern, scientific per-spective, some of the ideas, such as that nature 'wants' us to be social, or has 'designed' us to be so, might seem problematic. But irrespective of that, the Stoic theory certainly makes us sit up and think about what a good life might comprise of.

Stoic cosmopolitanism developed the metaphor of the human race as a 'body': as all the limbs contribute to the health of our body, so too does each human, like a limb, contribute to the body of humanity. The task for the Stoic, then, is to live out an aspiration to contribute to the common good, and for our belief-sets to be based on the implications of understanding oneself as a *civis mundi*, or 'citizen of the world'. In practice this meant, as first Epictetus, and then Marcus Aurelius, put it:

'To treat nothing as a matter of private profit, nor to plan about anything as though a detached unit, but to act like the foot or the hand, which, if they had the faculty of reason and understood the constitution of nature, would never exercise choice or desire in any other way but by reference to the whole.' *Discourses*, 2.10.

'For we are made for co-operation, like feet, like hands, like eyelids, like the rows of the upper and lower teeth. To act against one another is contrary to nature.' *Meditations*, 2.1.

Does this seem too high an ideal? Almost certainly, but a Stoic would probably respond that because we *are* social beings, these aims are also something on which our happiness depends. Put another way: if we are indeed social beings, then how could egoism, as we understand it, lead to happiness? It cannot! Indeed, the human being arrives at flourishing only through cultivating his social nature. Epictetus explains this as follows:

'...such is the nature of the animal man; everything that he does is for himself. Why, even the sun does everything for its own sake, and, for that matter, so does Zeus himself. But when Zeus wishes to be "Rain-bringer", and "Fruit-giver", and "Father of men and of gods", you can see for yourself that he cannot achieve these works, or win these appellations, unless he proves himself useful to the common interest; and in general he has so constituted the nature of the rational animal man, that he can attain nothing of his own proper goods unless he contributes something to the common interest. Hence it follows that it can no longer be unsocial for a man to do everything for his own sake.' *Discourses,* 1.19.

The analogy with Zeus, who is also 'Nature', is key: Nature, just by being itself, actively contributes to the common good. When Nature brings forth rain or fruit, everything is benefitted through these actions. This gives an added social dimension to what it means to 'live in accordance with Zeus or Nature': to live in accordance with nature is to be social. And, because this is *natural,* it allows for each person's nature to be fulfilled. Marcus Aurelius, similarly, compares the natural goodness the vine brings to others *just by doing its own thing* with the benevolent social being, doing one good deed after another, seeking no further reward than the performance of the act itself:

'Like the vine that produces its grapes, seeking nothing more once it has given forth its fruit...so the good man having done one deed well, does not shout it about, but turns to the next good deed, just like the vine turns to bear forth its fruit in due season.' *Meditations,* 5.6.

Epictetus's paradoxical claim, that *it can no longer be unsocial for a man to do everything for his own sake,* is, in short, based on the observation that only by cultivating good will towards others can the human being find happiness.

And how does the key aspect of Stoicism, namely the aspiration to live a life of virtue, fit into this picture? Is valuing virtue as 'the only good' all about going around in a 'virtuous bubble', as Stoicism is sometimes caricatured?

Hardly. For the Stoics, virtue is not something that happens in isolation. In order to come to fruition, virtue or 'the good' needs to be embedded in your social relationships. For the Stoic, it is 'up to her' to consider relationships with others the ground for virtuous action. Often, people panic about Stoicism when they read Epictetus say something like 'My father is nothing to me! He is not a good!' but this panic is misplaced as what Epictetus instead recommends is that one should value *being a good son to your father*. What is at the core of this distinction? As with everything else, it relates to Epictetus's focus on what is 'up to us': your father, in and of himself, is not under your control (as you may have noticed!), whereas your end of your relationship with him is under your control. And when this change of attitude occurs across your social relations, the shift will be to valuing primarily, therefore, one's role as a good friend, good parent and so on. Epictetus characterizes this shift in the following way:

> 'For where one can say "I" and "mine", to there will the human being incline. If "I" and "mine" are placed in the flesh, there will the human being's ruling power be; if they are in the moral purpose, there must it be; if they are in externals, there must it be. *If, therefore, I am where my moral purpose is, then, and then only, will I be the friend and son and father that I should be.* For then this will my interest – to keep my good faith, my self-respect, my forbearance, my co-cooperation, and to maintain my relationships with other human beings.' *Discourses, 2.22.*

It is only when one values the 'good' above all things, that, paradoxically, one can be the best father, friend, or daughter: only then does it become in one's *own* interest to keep one's integrity and good will towards your friends and family. And doing this, in turn, is what allows one's inherently social nature to flourish in the best possible way. The Stoic conception of 'virtue' itself, therefore, is strongly social.

In conclusion, some scholars, such as Mary Midgley, consider that the emergence of morality itself stems from human beings having a 'social instinct'. It would seem like the Stoics were one of the first, if not *the* first, to develop a rather universalist, whole-scale system of ethics based on that instinct. It is one of the most striking aspects of their thinking, and one which can never lose its relevance. To end, I quote one of Marcus's most famous reflections on Stoic cosmopolitanism. As I noted at the start, whether or not you agree with the idea that we are all, by nature, fundamentally social beings, this passages forces us to consider a most fundamental set of questions: *what does it mean to be a human being and what is good for the human being?*

> 'Whenever, as the sun rises, you feel unwilling to get up, have this thought ready to hand:
>
> "I rise to do the work of a human being"
>
> Why feel any resentment, when I am rising to do that for which I was born, for which I was brought into the world? Or was I made instead just to lie under these bedclothes, all warm and comfortable? "Well it is pleasurable to do so!" But were you born for pleasure? Look at it this way: were you born for passivity or to be a man of action? Can you not see that even the shrubs, sparrows, ants, spiders and bees all do their bit, their part in making up the smooth functioning of the universe? So why don't you do your bit too, and perform the role of a human being?' *Meditations* 5.1., my translation.

References

Midgley, M., *The Origin of Ethics* in Ed. Singer, P., 'A Companion to Ethics'. Wiley- Blackwell: 1993.

STOICS ARE NOT UNEMOTIONAL!

Donald Robertson

The misconception that Stoics are unemotional like robots, or like the Vulcan "Mister Spock" in Star Trek, is widespread today, and yet not one that was shared so easily by the ancients [*See also Jen Farren's piece, 'Stoicism and Star Trek', in Part VIII*]. In contrast, other philosophies were made to bear the brunt of the joke. For example, the founder of Greek Skepticism, Pyrrho of Elis, was jokingly said to be so apathetic, in the sense of being 'indifferent to the world', that his followers had to chase around after him to prevent him walking off cliffs or into the path of speeding horse-drawn wagons. That joke was never made about the Stoics because, by contrast, they were well-known for their active engagement in family life and politics. Likewise, the Epicureans made the attainment of tranquillity, or the avoidance of pain, their goal of life, and saw no intrinsic value in fellowship with other human beings. This often led them to withdraw from politics or family life, and even to live in relative seclusion. By contrast, the Stoics, for whom tranquillity is good *only* when it accompanies the virtues of wisdom and justice, believed that fellowship with the rest of mankind is natural and fundamental to the goal of life, which entails "living in agreement" with reason, the Nature of the universe, and the rest of mankind. In fact, the founding text of Stoicism, Zeno's *Republic*, centred on his "dream" of an ideal Stoic society, consisting of enlightened and benevolent friends, living in harmony together, under the patronage of Eros, the god of love.

For Epictetus, it was the Stoic concept of "appropriate action" in our familial and civil relationships, and the emphasis on acting justly and philanthropically, which laid to rest the misconception that the Stoics were aloof and unemotional (*Discourses*, 3.2). The Stoics believed that we are essentially rational and *social* animals who experience a feeling of "natural affection" for those closest to us, which it is natural and rational to extend to the rest of mankind, forming the basis of an attitude sometimes called Stoic "philanthropy". However, by placing value on others, even in a somewhat detached manner, Stoics also open themselves up to a variety of naturally-occurring emotional reactions, including distress when valued things appear to be threatened. According to the ancient Stoics, even the perfect Sage feels natural affection, or love for other human beings, and is not completely insensitive to other feelings that naturally follow from maintaining these affectionate social relationships. Marcus Aurelius surely loved his notoriously wayward son Commodus, while accepting that it was ultimately beyond his control to remedy completely his heir's folly and his vicious character.

Indeed, Marcus described the ideal Stoic character, as exemplified by his own teacher, Sextus of Chaerona, as being "full of love and yet free from passion". For Marcus, Sextus was full of "natural affection" or "family affection" – the kind of love parents have for their children. But Stoics did not stop there. They also sought to emulate Zeus, the father of mankind, by extending their natural affection to the whole of humanity. This dilutes the emotion and prevents it from becoming an infatuation with any individual, or an irrational "passion" of the kind they sought to free themselves from. Hence also the Stoic focus on *apatheia*, which, in the Stoic context, means the absence of irrational, unhealthy, or excessive "passions". As we'll see, the Stoics repeatedly emphasised that by this they did not mean "apathy" or complete lack of feeling for other people.

But let's see what the Stoics themselves say about 'apatheia'. After describing the Stoic theory of irrational passions, Diogenes Laertius wrote of the founders of Stoicism, probably meaning either Zeno or Chrysippus:

'They say the wise man is also without passions (*apathê*), because he is not vulnerable to them. But the bad man is called "without passions" in a different sense, which means the same as "hard-hearted" and "insensitive".' *Lives of the Philosophers*, 7.117.

Epictetus says something quite similar, that Stoics ought not to be free from passions (*apathê*) in the sense of being unfeeling "like a statue", but rather that they should focus on "appropriate actions" and maintaining one's natural and acquired relationships, as a family member and a citizen (*Discourses*, 3.2). In addition, Cicero portrays the Stoic Laelius as saying that it would be the greatest possible mistake to try to eliminate feelings of friendship, because even animals experience natural affection for their offspring. This natural affection was shared across the animal world and was something which Stoics viewed as the foundation of human love and friendship as well (*Laelius*, 13). We would not only be *dehumanising* ourselves by eliminating natural affection between friends, he says, but reducing ourselves below animal nature to something more like a mere tree-trunk or stone.

Likewise, Seneca argues that the virtues of courage and self-discipline appear to require that the Stoic Sage must actually *experience* something akin to fear and desire – otherwise he has no feelings to overcome. A brave man is not someone who doesn't experience any trace of fear whatsoever but someone who acts courageously *despite* feeling anxiety. A man who has great self-discipline or restraint is not someone who feels no inkling of desire but someone who overcomes his cravings by abstaining from acting upon them. Seneca writes:

'There are misfortunes which strike the sage – without incapacitating him, of course – such as physical pain, infirmity, the loss of friends or children, or the catastrophes of his country when it is devastated by war. I grant that he is sensitive to these things, for we do not impute to him the hardness of a rock or iron. There is no virtue in putting up with that which one does not feel.' *On the Constancy of the Sage,* 10.4.

The Stoic ideal is not to be "passionless" (*apathê*) in the sense of being "apathetic", "hard-hearted", "insensitive" or "like a statue" of stone or iron. Rather, it is to experience natural affection for ourselves, our loved-ones, and other human beings, and to value our lives in accord with nature, which arguably opens us up to experiencing emotional reactions to loss or frustration. Seneca elsewhere explains that whereas the Epicureans mean "a mind immune to feeling" when they speak of *apatheia*, this "unfeelingness" is actually the opposite of what the Stoics mean (*Letters*, 9): "This is the difference between us Stoics and the Epicureans; our wise man overcomes every discomfort but feels it, their wise man does not even feel it."

The virtue of the Sage consists in his ability to endure painful feelings and rise above them, with magnanimity, while continuing to maintain his relationships and interaction with the world.

Similar themes are covered in more detail in *Stoicism and The Art of Happiness: Teach Yourself*, by Donald Robertson, published by Hodder & Stoughton, 2013.

ON THE MOTIVATIONS OF A STOIC

Michel Daw

As humans, we require basic needs to function. We can speak of being 'rational', but in reality, we require a functioning body to think clearly. To borrow from Abraham Maslow, the American psychologist, we need to have our physical, social, safety and other important needs met before we can even consider attempting the so-called 'self-actualization' of the rational mind.

But once those needs are met, what are the motivations of a Stoic? There are several layers to consider.

The first, of course, is Virtue. We must remember that virtue is not something that one merely has, but is something that must be *done*. In order to have virtue, we must *be* virtuous; we must be courageous in the face of challenges, we must be just in the distribution of goods and rights, we must be temperate in our dealings as well as our acquisitions, and most of all we must be wise in our choices of action.

Secondly, we need to remember that when the Stoics speak of 'indifferents', they mean things that, in their nature, have no *moral* value. Nevertheless, they have other kinds of value. Good food and clothing, shelter and safety: things like these have great *physical* value. Relationships, friends, art, music: these things have great *emotional* value. Books, education, conversation: these things have a great *intellectual* value. And while Virtue alone is in my control, these other things are to be pursued and managed by virtuous means.

Third, while I must remember that as a Stoic I am in control only of my own actions, I am also part of a family, a community, a country. I am human, and being human means that all ideas of individuality are an illusion. The food we eat, the clothes we wear, the very language we speak that forms the framework of our thinking, are all inheritances of the culture and species which we are bound to support in return. We see this idea expressed in Hierocles's "concentric circles". In these circles, your mind forms the centre, whilst the next circle stands for your immediate family, the next for brothers and sisters, the next for aunts and uncles, all the way to your city, country and finally the entire human race, the aim being for us to 'lessen the gap' between us and each of these 'circles'.

So what is it that motivates us? It is just this: remembering all three things together is the key. We must not only care for ourselves, but see to it that those who are in our care and our responsibility are provided with the same level of care. We must do so for all of us. We cannot speak of being Stoic, without being just, courageous, temperate and wise. And we cannot be those things if we stand idly by while our brothers and sisters are unable even to reach for the so-called lofty rational heights we dream of for ourselves.

I realize that this is an unpopular view amongst those who see in Stoicism only the opportunity to justify cutting themselves off from the rest of humanity or worse, from their own emotional life. But Stoicism is about Joy, Serenity, Meaning and Purpose. It is about being a useful and important member of society.

In short, it is about being an excellent human being, and part of a race of beings that has the potential for greatness.

PART TWO: ADAPTING STOICISM FOR THE MODERN DAY

WHICH STOICISM?

John Sellars

The aim of the 'Stoicism Today' project is to highlight ways in which ancient Stoicism might be of use to people as a general guide to life or might contribute to a therapeutic response to specific problems. Some critics might object that the version of Stoicism being offered bears little relation to the Hellenistic philosophy founded by Zeno and developed by Chrysippus and others (see e.g. Williams on Nussbaum (*LRB* 16/20 (20 Oct. 1994), 25-6) and Warren on Irvine (*Polis* 26/1 (2009), 176-9)). As Williams quipped, what use is Chrysippus' logical theory in learning how to live?

This project, by contrast, has been inspired primarily by a study of Marcus Aurelius and the materials prepared for the project draw on the works of Seneca, Musonius Rufus, and Epictetus – all later Roman Stoics. This is not just because the works of these later Stoics survive and those of the earlier Stoics active in Athens do not; it also reflects the fact that these later Stoics focus their attention on what we might call 'Stoic practice'. They offer a wide range of practical guidance designed to contribute towards the cultivation of tranquillity or what Zeno called 'a smooth flow of life'. It is hard to know to what extent these sorts of practices figured in early Stoicism: we know that early Stoics wrote books on mental training (*askêsis*) and we also know that this featured prominently in Cynicism, an important influence on the early Stoics. Ultimately the evidence is just too thin for us to know for sure.

It may be that this concern with practices (what Pierre Hadot called 'spiritual exercises') did not figure much in early Stoicism and it may have been a Pythagorean theme in later Stoicism introduced by the Roman Stoic Sextius, who influenced Seneca. That view would hold that there is a marked difference between early Hellenistic Stoicism and later Roman Stoicism (although in my own book *Stoicism* (2006) I consciously tried to downplay such a division by treating the ancient Stoic tradition as a continuous whole). But even if one did take that view, the later Roman Stoics were indeed Stoics – they self identified as Stoics and others in antiquity described them as Stoics. If their use of practices counts as an innovation in the history of ancient Stoicism that does not stop them being fully paid up members of the Stoic tradition. The Stoicism that the 'Stoicism Today Project' draws on is this later variety of Roman Stoicism.

Having said that, it may be that the difference between early and later Stoicism is not as marked as some may think. As I have already noted, ultimately it is hard to know for sure given the fragmentary nature of the evidence for the early Stoa but we do know that the Cynics engaged in these sorts of practices and recent scholarship has rightly stressed the Cynic influence on all the early Stoics (e.g. Goulet-Cazé's *Les Kynica du stoïcisme*, 2003). If the Cynic teachers of the early Stoics engaged in these practices and later Roman Stoics did too then it is not unreasonable to think that the early Stoics in between might have also, although we cannot know for sure.

Even so, the 'Stoicism Today' project is primarily concerned with drawing on the surviving works of the later Roman Stoics who do outline a variety of practices designed to cultivate well-being. The project could have been called 'Roman Stoicism Today', but 'Stoicism Today' is far from misleading.

There is a separate question about the extent to which it makes sense to call these practices 'Stoic' if they are divorced from the rest of Stoic philosophy. Are these practices essentially Stoic or only contingently so to the extent that later Stoics happened to make use of them? My own view is that these practices only count as philosophical practices when done in the light of some of the central tenets of Stoic philosophy – especially their theory of value and perhaps also their determinism. However one of the striking features of the Roman Stoics – Epictetus to an extent, Marcus Aurelius even more so – is the thought that these practices can benefit people even if they are not yet fully committed to the full range of Stoic doctrines. The beginning student, suggests Epictetus, can benefit from these practices before they have studied the full range of Stoic doctrine, and the cautious student of Nature, Marcus says, can pursue well-being even if they remain unsure whether Nature is governed by providence or is merely chaotic.

In short, the Roman Stoics offer a helpful model of how one might start to draw on these Stoic practices even if one is not yet fully committed to the Stoic philosophical system. One might say that simply embracing some of these practices does not make someone a Stoic if they do not also embrace all of the doctrine, and that is fine: the aim of the project is not to create a new sect of doctrinaire Stoics but rather the more modest goal of drawing on Stoic practices to the extent they might help people in their everyday lives.

References

Goulet-Cazé, M-O., *Les Kynica du stoïcisme*, Franz Steiner Verlag, 2003.

Hadot, P., *Philosophy as a Way of Life*. Blackwell, 1995.

Sellars, J., *Stoicism*. University of California Press, 2006.

Warren, J., Review of William B. Irvine, *A Guide to the Good Life*, *Polis* 26/1 (2009), 176-79.

Williams, B., 'Do Not Disturb', *London Review of Books* 16/20 (20 Oct. 1994), 25-26.

A SIMPLIFIED MODERN APPROACH TO STOICISM

Donald Robertson

In this article, I present a simplified set of Stoic psychological practices, that could both act as a 'daily philosophical routine' and as a very concise introduction to Stoicism as a way of life. Whilst Chrysippus, the third head of the Stoic school, wrote over 700 books fleshing out Stoic ideas and adding complex arguments to support them, its founder, Zeno of Citium, expressed his doctrines in notoriously terse arguments and concise maxims. In this article, my aim is to present a concise version, but keep in mind that there is, of course, a complex philosophy lurking in the background.

Both Seneca and Epictetus refer to the *Golden Verses of Pythagoras*, a text which provides a good framework for developing a daily routine, book-ended by morning and evening contemplative practices. A key Stoic idea which also informed these practices, and which was also at the core of Epictetus's philosophy, was that: '...to become educated (in Stoic philosophy) means just this: to learn what things are our own, and what are not' (*Discourses*, 4.5.7). The practical consequence of this distinction is essentially quite simple: 'What, then, is to be done? To make the best of what is in our power, and take the rest as it naturally happens' (*Discourses*, 1.1.17).

The routine below is designed to provide an introduction to Stoic practice for the 21st Century, which can lead naturally into a wider appreciation of Stoic philosophy as a way of life. The instructions are designed to be as straightforward and concise as possible, while still remaining reasonably faithful to classical Stoicism.

The Basic Philosophical Routine

Stage 1: Morning Preparation

Plan your day ahead with the Stoic "reserve clause" in mind, that is to say: decide what goals you want to achieve in advance and make a decision to try to achieve them but with the caveat: "Fate permitting." In other words, aim for success and pursue it wholeheartedly while also being prepared to accept setbacks or failure with equanimity, insofar as they lie outside of your direct control. Try to choose your goals wisely, picking things that are rational and healthy for you to pursue. Your *primary goal* throughout these three stages should be to protect and improve your fundamental wellbeing, particularly in terms of your character and ability to think clearly about your life. You're going to try to do this by cultivating greater self-awareness and practical wisdom, which requires setting goals for yourself that are healthy, while pursuing them in a sort of "detached" way, without being particularly attached to the outcome.

Stage 2: Stoic Mindfulness (Prosoche) Throughout the Day

Throughout the day, continually pay attention to the way you make value-judgements and respond to your thoughts. Be mindful, in particular of the way you respond to strong emotions or desires. When you experience a distressing or problematic thought, pause, and tell yourself: "This is just a thought and not at all the thing it claims to represent." Remind yourself that it is not things that upset you but your judgements about things. Where appropriate, rather than being carried away by your initial impressions, try to postpone responding to them for at least an hour, waiting until your feelings have settled down and you are able to view things more calmly and objectively before deciding what action to take.

43

Once you have achieved greater self-awareness of your stream of consciousness and the ability to take a step back from your thoughts in this way, begin also to apply a simple standard of evaluation to your thoughts and impressions as follows. Having paused to view your thoughts from a distance, ask yourself whether they are about things that are directly under your control or things that are not. This has been called the general precept or strategy of ancient Stoic practice. If you notice that your feelings are about something that's outside of your direct control then respond by trying to accept the fact that it's out of your hands, saying to yourself: "This is nothing to me." Focus your attention instead on doing what is within your sphere of control with wisdom and to the best of your ability, regardless of the actual outcome. In other words, remind yourself to apply the reserve clause described above to each situation. Look for ways to remind yourself of this. For example, the *Serenity Prayer* is a well-known version of this idea, which you might want to memorise or write down somewhere and contemplate each day:

'Give me the Serenity to accept
the things I cannot change,
The Courage to change the things I can,
And the Wisdom to know the difference.'

Stage 3: Night-time Review

Review your whole day, three times, if possible, before going to sleep. Focus on the key events and the order in which they happened, e.g., the order in which you undertook different tasks or interacted with different people during the day. Some questions you might ask yourself are:

– What did you do that was good for your fundamental wellbeing? (What went well?)
– What did you do that harmed your fundamental wellbeing? (What went badly?)

– What opportunities did you miss to do something good for your fundamental wellbeing? (What was omitted?)

Counsel yourself as if you were advising a close friend or loved one. What can you learn from the day and, where appropriate, how can you do better in the future? Praise yourself for what went well and allow yourself to reflect on it with satisfaction. You may also find it helps to give yourself a simple subjective rating (from 0-10) to measure how consistently you followed the instructions here or how good you were at pursuing rational and healthy goals while remaining detached from things outside of your direct control. However, try to be concise in your evaluation of things and to arrive at conclusions without ruminating over things for too long.

WHAT CAN THE STOICS DO FOR US?

Antonia Macaro

Stoicism is not short of fans these days. Apart from cropping up in a number of books on popular philosophy, it is not infrequent to come across their ideas in all sorts of mainstream publications – *The Guardian*, *Prospect*, *Psychologies*, not to mention *The Philosophers' Magazine*. This is not too surprising as especially the later texts by the Roman Stoics – Seneca, Epictetus, Marcus Aurelius – are full of wonderfully apt advice on how to live. Far from the abstractions of some moral philosophy, which often gives little assistance on how to lead a good life, Stoic authors wrote about daily concerns, and so gained lasting relevance for many people.

Yet, if you started delving into Stoic literature, you might find some of the advice repugnant, even shocking. In Epictetus, for instance, you would find this exhortation: 'If you kiss your child, or your wife, say to yourself that it is a human being that you are kissing; and then you will not be disturbed if either of them dies' (*Handbook*, §3). As for Marcus Aurelius, you would be told that sex should be thought of as 'something rubbing against your penis, a brief seizure and a little cloudy liquid' (*Meditations*, 6.13). Is Stoicism a life-affirming philosophy that can truly help us to live better lives in the modern world or a fiercely radical perspective, intriguing but too remote and demanding to have any real relevance to our daily conduct? Or both?

Stoicism is a complex philosophy in which ethics was an integral part of a tightly woven system that also included logic and what they called physics but is clearly more what we would now call metaphysics. John Sellars, senior philosophy lecturer and author of *The Art of Living*, explains, in conversation, that Stoic physics involved the idea of a 'divine rational mind that pervades all of nature, which is the soul of the world, and which all our individual souls are fragments of. A lot of Stoic arguments about how we should respond to fate, and particularly bad fortune, is predicated on the thought that there is this divine providential mind organising the whole process.'

These metaphysical views have ethical consequences. Our bodies and possessions are mere matter, but our power of rational choice partakes of divine rationality. This is what marks humans apart from other creatures, and it is the only thing that should be valued unconditionally. In Epictetus's stark formulation, 'In our own power are choice and all actions dependent on choice; not in our power are the body, the parts of the body, property, parents, brothers, children, country, and, in short, all with whom we associate. Where, then, shall we place the good? To what class of things shall we apply it? To that of things that are in our own power'.

If we wished to live a Stoic life, therefore, we would need to concentrate on exercising rational choice, which is the only thing that is truly up to us, and learn to challenge any initial judgements that mislead us with the appearance of value. The emotions and desires stirred in us by the things we mistakenly regard as valuable in life are avoidable disturbances and impediments to leading the rational life, and should be eradicated. We should constantly remind ourselves that anything befalling us that does not pertain to the sphere of choice and action is not in our power, so we should follow our destiny without complaint. Like a dog tied to a cart, in Epictetus's analogy, we can either choose to trot behind it willingly or be dragged kicking and screaming.

We would still be allowed to pursue our natural inclinations to some extent, however, since the Stoics attributed a degree of value to what they called 'preferred indifferents' – things we would rather have than not. Richard Sorabji, Emeritus Professor of philosophy and author of *Emotion and Peace of Mind* among many other books, points out, in conversation, that 'by Antipater's time (2nd century BCE) they are saying that it is your duty to do everything in your power to secure these natural objectives, for yourself and for other people.' But our primary allegiance must always be to our rationality. Epictetus reminds us that 'the good is thus preferred above every form of relationship. My father is nothing to me, only the good. – Are you so hard-hearted? – Such is my nature, and such is the coin which god has given me.' No wonder the Stoic sage (sophos) was a more or less mythical figure.

So what are the problems with adopting Stoicism as a modern philosophy of life? One worry is that a lot of its foundational beliefs, such as the ideas that our rationality is a fragment of the divine, or that emotions are disturbances created by false attributions of value, clash with what we in fact know about the world. Therefore any advice based on these beliefs might be misguided. Recent findings in neuroscience, for instance, show that far from always being a hindrance to reason, emotions are an integral part of it. We evolved to have emotions for good reason, and without them it is hard to navigate one's way through life. Of course emotions can also get us into trouble, and frequently they do, but the answer is most certainly not to eradicate them (even if that were possible).

The Stoic theory of value has been explicitly rejected by two leading academics in the field, Martha Nussbaum and Richard Sorabji. When I talk to Sorabji he soon mentions the 'unacceptable face of Stoicism', which he steers clear of. I ask him whether he agrees with Epictetus's advice about aiming not to be distressed when bereaved, and he says: 'No, it's best to be absolutely shattered, because the rest of your life would otherwise have been spent in this detached way, always thinking "I'm kissing a mortal". It can't be good. How could it be a good life to spend most of it detached from the

48

people you're closest to just so that you don't suffer some years of distress at some point? That can't be a sensible equation.' He acknowledges that disowning this aspect of Stoic doctrine leaves him as vulnerable as anyone else to grief, 'but there's an even bigger price I would pay if I did buy it', he says.

We have also learned from studies in psychology that our awareness of and control over our own attitudes, motives and intentions is much more limited than we might have hoped, and that context plays a large part in influencing our actions. It is reasonable to believe that we have a certain amount of control, and that this can be increased, but it would be foolish to convince ourselves that we are endowed with anything like full rationality and complete freedom to choose how to respond to things. In fact, our freedom may be fairly limited.

Given all this, could anybody nowadays really accept Stoicism as a whole system? Actually, yes. Keith Seddon, director of the Stoic Foundation and author of *Stoic Serenity*, is a practising Stoic. Nor is he the only one, as there seems to be a thriving Stoic community to be found online, with groups like the New Stoa and the International Stoic Forum. What Seddon discovered in Stoicism seemed to him to chime with a kind of mystical experience he had at 19: 'When I was looking up at the trees I had for those few minutes an apprehension of everything, and what that meant was simply that everything is connected together.' So when he read what the Stoics had to say about 'chains of cause and effect, and how fate is the complex pattern of cause and effect right through the entire history of the world, encompassing everything that happens', he could connect these theories with the experience he'd had. Furthermore, what he thought he apprehended was that 'the connections themselves constituted the rational agency that creates the whole thing'.

For Seddon, being a Stoic means emphasising 'the way you do things, not what you do'. He makes a 'distinction between how you are as an agent and what you do in terms of your undertakings. Things can happen that interfere with your doing the thing, but it's doing the thing it's interfering with, not you as the rational agent, because what you are as a rational agent is independent of what you do.' Our projects can be ruined by external circumstances, we 'don't have control necessarily over things – "let's hope for the best" is really the most you can say – but that doesn't affect the agent that you are, which is separate from the things you do', he says. What we then need to do is to fulfill the roles that are thrown our way to the best of our ability. In his case, one of the roles that has been thrown in his way is that of carer of his wife, who is disabled.

He even accepts the theory of value, saying that 'if you can accept the general principle that the only good thing is virtue or behaving excellently or trying to behave excellently and the only bad thing is being pressured into vice of one sort or another – being dishonest, being unkind, selfish – then if somebody dies, even if they're close to me, it can't actually make me do anything bad, so in that sense I'm safe. Something's happened that I don't want to happen, that I prefer not to happen. The theory says that I shouldn't go so far as to say it's actually a bad thing.'

Perhaps it's a question of emphasising certain things and toning down others. And, of course, of choosing our Stoics. With later Stoics, Sorabji tells me, the focus shifts from the sage, who couldn't do anything wrong, to imperfect beings like you and me. Panaetius, for instance, 'said "we Stoics have been talking about what the ideal person would look like, and we've been criticised because there hasn't been an ideal person, so let's talk about ordinary people – if they have a little bit of good character, wouldn't that be a good thing?" Because it was explicitly said up to that point, if you're not totally virtuous you're totally vicious.' But from the late 2nd century BCE there's 'more and more attention to the idea that you may have made a little progress towards having a good character. And that makes a wonderful difference, because it makes Stoicism 'an ethical philosophy which taps you on the shoulder. And what other ethical system can claim that?' A good example is that of Seneca's letters, which address questions that are bound to have concerned most of us at some point.

Sellars points out that certainly by the time of Marcus Aurelius there is less reliance on a providential plan being in place and more emphasis on the idea that 'we should simply accept by virtue of us being finite beings that some things are going to be out of our control, and our ethical task is to find a way of dealing with those things in a positive way.' So Marcus stresses 'his finite and limited status within the world, the lack of power and control he has over things, the extent to which he finds himself thrown into a situation that wasn't of his choosing and now he simply has to decide how best to act and how to do best by the situation and by himself given the circumstances.'

But if we want to avail ourselves of the wealth of advice in Stoicism while hanging on to what we know about the world our best bet may be a 'pick and choose' approach. This was endorsed by the Stoics themselves, says Sorabji. 'The third and most famous of the early Stoics, Chrysippus', for instance, 'said he was perfectly willing to help people with their emotions even if they didn't share Stoic beliefs.' And that's how Sorabji uses Stoic philosophy too: 'rather eclectically – I choose the bits which I find helpful and I don't take the full theory.'

And yet, this approach is not entirely unproblematic either. First of all, we need to decide what to choose and on what grounds, especially if we have given up the metaphysical foundations. According to Sorabji, this is not so difficult: 'Try it. It takes a bit of time to get into a habit, perhaps. But try it out.' The claim that we can find useful advice in Seneca's letters, for instance, is easily tested by reading Seneca's letters. And 'although I'm taking only a modest part of Stoicism, it's not modest in its effects. I think it has wonderful effects.' Agreed. But it can be difficult to know what advice to appropriate and what to reject unless we have some conception of the good life. If we haven't thought this through, we might end up with the wrong bits of advice.

If, for instance, we have accepted the advice to put inner tranquillity above all else, we might be tempted to avoid getting emotionally close to people for fear of future suffering. This may not be the best plan if we wish to have a fulfilling life, as Sorabji clearly stated, as it could lead to an impoverished life narrowly focussed on avoiding pain. Yes, tranquillity is a good thing. But it should not necessarily trump all other values. So when we follow Stoic advice we need to be at least aware of the danger of smuggling in more Stoic metaphysics than we had bargained for. From everything we know about psychology it is understanding and managing emotions, not eradicating them, that is more likely to help us to live a good life.

Another danger, ever-present in popular references to Stoicism, is that of pruning so much that its spirit is lost or subverted. For example, Epictetus's view that 'it is not the things themselves that disturb people but their judgements about those things' is often quoted as the foundation on which CBT (Cognitive-Behaviour Therapy) and REBT (Rational-Emotive Behaviour Therapy) are built. It is true that Aaron Beck and Albert Ellis, respective founders of these therapies, were influenced by Stoic ideas. And there is certainly an overlap, if only in the basic idea that 'to have an emotional response to something does require a cognitive process', as Seddon says. 'There is a family resemblance', comments John Sellars, adding that 'ultimately everyone's problems are the product of the way in which they think about themselves and the world, and if they analyse their judgements, which they can do through philosophy or [some] form of psychotherapy, then they can make different judgements which will literally transform the way in which they interact with the world, the values they have, the emotions they have, everything.'

But it would be misleading to overstate the similarities. CBT and REBT aim at helping people to overcome troublesome emotions by modifying their beliefs. The ultimate goal is that of relieving clients' distress. Like most other modern psychotherapies, they are hands-off about what clients should value in life. Stoicism, on the other hand, was a radical philosophy that aimed at restructuring the aspiring Stoic's worldview. It was indeed conceived of as a kind of therapy for the soul, but like other forms of ancient therapy it was 'didactic and moralistic'. It is in a way ironic to use Stoic ideas, which drastically redefined the good life, in the service of a conventional notion of happiness, of an unexamined 'feeling good'.

One thing is not in doubt, however, and that is that there is indeed a lot of useful advice to be found in the Stoic literature, which can assist us to live better if we are a bit discriminating. So what might the Stoics be especially well placed to help us with?

Three things, says Sorabji. One is their 'advice about how not to get emotionally worked up completely needlessly about everyday things. I accept that's a small part of what they thought about emotions, but they would have approved, I think. The second area is the idea of thinking about who you are and who you want to be in making decisions in life. The third area is [what they say regarding] our weaknesses and foibles. I haven't found any ethics, ancient or modern, that's as good as that. They are only three little patches of Stoicism, but they are terribly important. Their importance is much greater than the proportion they form of what Stoicism is.'

For Seddon, on the other hand, 'the main thing is to follow Epictetus's teaching, which is to be aware of what is external and what is internal, so it's not what happens that matters, it's how I engage with what happens that matters. Another way of saying that is: there's a power of agency that I have that is what I am, and then I have my projects; circumstances and other people can harm my undertakings but they can't harm me. That's something that you can begin to maintain as a constant mindfulness in the course of doing things.' So if you're frightened of something, for example, you might think to yourself, 'that's external to me, it's not in my control; I'll just do what I have to do to be a good person, and that's the best I can ever do.'

Most of us could probably benefit from adopting Stoic perspectives like questioning what is really valuable in life, reminding ourselves that a lot of the things we commonly worry about are not that important; the habit of scrutinising our emotions, remembering that we can have a degree of influence on how we feel by changing how we think; and accepting that much of what happens to us in life is beyond our control.

Particularly useful is the advice to keep the fragility of life at the front of our mind. The Stoics have bequeathed us several exercises for this purpose, as one of their central methods was that of anticipating future disasters – a practice intriguingly divergent from the currently ubiquitous advice to be optimistic. Seneca for instance advises 'to envisage every possibility and to strengthen the spirit to deal with the things which may conceivably come about. Rehearse them in your mind: exile, torture, war, shipwreck.' While the traditional aim of the exercise was to remind ourselves that the things that could be taken away from us (which is everything apart from reason) should mean nothing to us, we could use it instead to help us to keep a sense of perspective and appreciate what we have (although we should bear in mind that unless this is done in the right spirit it could lead to anxiety and depression rather than tranquillity).

At the same time, it would probably not make for a good life to adopt the view that emotions are disturbances to be eradicated, or that nothing outside our control should be valued, or that perfect rationality is an achievable goal. As Sorabji recognises, when 'you're picking and choosing, inevitably there is this distortion – quite a serious distortion. You could say I wasn't a Stoic, because I believe in emotion.' 'It's good to have an historical understanding at the same time', he adds.

And that is the main point. It's fine to pick and choose so long as we do our homework and think through what we are taking, what we are leaving and why. If we don't, and are not aware that taking on too much Stoicism may not be good for our flourishing, we could end up with some seriously bad advice about how to run our lives.

This article was first published in *The Philosophers' Magazine,* issue 49, 2nd quarter, 2010.

PART THREE: STOIC ADVICE

ON DEATH ACCEPTANCE

Corey Anton

Like many philosophical systems in the ancient word, the Stoic tradition makes no lofty bid for an afterlife nor does it instruct us to despise death. Death is outside of one's control, and accordingly, it must be dealt with by indifference. It is accepted as part of the meaning of life, as something that Divine Providence saw to be fitting. In *Discourses* 2.6, we find Epictetus admonishing us from trying to take under our control what is beyond it: "… know that you are cursing men when you pray for them not to die: it is like a prayer not to be ripened, not to be reaped." And in *The Handbook* §14 he writes, "It is silly to want your children…and your friends to live forever, for that means that you want what is not in your control to be in your control, and what is not yours to be yours." Not only is the fact of death beyond our control, Providence saw fit that humans can have no knowledge of anything beyond life. We are to act with regard to *this world*, meeting our duties with courage and goodwill and accepting whatever happens.

As fundamentally beyond our control, death is something to which we should be indifferent, although admittedly the wise may learn how to use death as a resource for gaining perspective and making decisions. In §21 of *The Handbook*, Epictetus advocates a nearness to death, if only to keep desire in its proper place: "Keep before your eyes from day to day death and exile and all things that seem terrible, but death most of all, and then you will never set your thoughts on what is low and will never desire anything beyond measure." Death too can be regarded as a gift insofar as we can know that we will die, which basically implies that we know that we cannot postpone decisions indefinitely; a time to act will come and then that moment will pass. By maintaining an image of death before us, we are reminded of what is and is not under our control. We are essentially, as Epictetus writes, "a tiny soul carrying around a corpse."

We also find Epictetus giving advice that brings together the Stoic demand of concerning ourselves only with what is under our control while also meeting the demand of social politeness and graciousness. Epictetus suggests that we can sympathize with someone who is grieving over the loss of a loved one, so long as we remember what it is that actually troubles people:

> 'When you see a man shedding tears in sorrow for a child abroad or dead, or for loss of property, be sure that you are not carried away by the impression that it is outward ills that make him miserable. Keep this thought with you: "What distresses him is not the event, for that does not distress another, but his judgment on the event." Therefore do not hesitate to sympathize with him as far as words go, and if it so chances, even to groan with him; but take heed that you do not also groan in your inner being.' *Handbook*, §16.

Death is not a bad thing. It only seems bad if we already assented to putting under our jurisdiction what is naturally beyond our power. Mortality simply makes sense; it had to come along for life to be what it is, and all of this is good.

Writing about the gift character of existence, Moses Hadas describes Seneca's views on death and death-acceptance. He suggest that once a fully Stoic view is adopted, a person reckons not only his chattels and property and position but even his body and eyes and hands, all that a man cherishes in life, even his own personality, as temporary holdings, and he lives as if he were on loan to himself, and is ready to return the whole sum cheerfully on demand…When the order to return the deposits comes he will not quarrel with Fortune but will say, "I am thankful for what I have held and enjoyed."

It is, in fact, only when we seek what is beyond our control that death becomes an issue. Imagine a spoiled child looking up at the nighttime sky, seeing the stars in the heavens, and the youth reaches up and tries to grab one. Witnessing such an event, a parent might tell the child that this is impossible, "You cannot touch the stars, but you can look at them." We can imagine the child's ungrateful reaction "I don't even want to see what I can't have; I'd just as soon banish the stars." And so, we too may be upset that we can have ideas of what we will never physically experience. Fortunately, we need not have life after death, for life itself is enough. We need not hold eternity in our hands. It is enough to merely glimpse eternity, to share in the *logos* and hence to be able to contemplate the Cosmos.

Ultimately, death poses no problem once we focus exclusively upon moral intention rather than ultimate achievement of any ends. Moral intention gives an act completeness from its very inception. As Pierre Hadot writes, "Even if the action which we are carrying out were in fact interrupted by death, this would not make it incomplete; for what gives an action its completeness is precisely the moral intention by which it is inspired, not the subject matter on which it is exercised." If we have lived right the entire time, all has been good. To live right is to give each day the completeness of the eternal.

GRATITUDE AND WONDER

Mark Garvey

Introduction: Each essay at Mark Garvey's blog, *Old Answers*, begins with a brief Q&A, in which an ancient philosopher responds to a query from a (typically vexed) modern-day seeker.

Q: *"When I was young, I was interested in everything, and the world was full of wonder. But adulthood has worn me down. With each passing day I feel more like Oscar Wilde's paradigmatic cynic: 'A man who knows the price of everything and the value of nothing.' This change in attitude happened while I wasn't looking, and I'm not happy about it. The only people I know who seem unjaded and reasonably content with their lot are religious believers, but the faith of my youth seems to have flown the coop. I'm bone-weary of the snark and cynicism that pass for social intercourse these days, especially on the internet. How can I take a step back, get a fresh view, and rekindle wonder in my life?"*

A: *"Any one thing in the creation is sufficient to demonstrate a Providence, to a humble and grateful mind. Not to instance great things, the mere possibility of producing milk from grass, cheese from milk, and wool from skins—who formed and planned this? No one, say you. O surprising irreverence and dullness!"* Epictetus, *Discourses*, 1.16.

Epictetus raises so many currently unfashionable ideas here—God (Providence), humility, reverence—that it's hard to know where to begin. For secular moderns, his expression of wonder at the seemingly miraculous origins of milk, cheese, and wool can easily provoke a smile of condescension, perhaps even a sneer. *The primitive naïveté!* What can such a man, bound by the limits of first-century cosmology, ignorant of today's materialist, scientistic gospel and the "blind" inexorability of natural selection—have to offer that could be of any use to iPhone-Age Man?

We can't read far in Epictetus without recognizing his belief in God. It's also impossible to imagine a topic in current culture that has been so thoroughly mangled, misrepresented, and misunderstood. "The God question," mankind's inherent itch to grapple with the ultimate mystery of existence, has, in recent years, played out on the internet, and in the publishing world, with all the subtleness and intellectual acuity of a Three Stooges pie fight. In the process, humanity's most complex, fertile, culture-shaping force—rich in wisdom traditions, creative arts, ethical thought, and psychological insight, and, for many, positively crackling with intimations of the transcendent—has been reduced to a tiresome shouting match, with doctrinaire literalists on one side and scorched-earth anti-theists on the other. To call this state of affairs regrettable doesn't begin to cover it.

I'm happy with Epictetus's theistic leanings. But whether or not we believe in God, it's important to guard against the occasional impulse, when we're sifting these ancient ideas, to toss out both baby and bathwater. History is replete with philosophies and belief systems that, despite arguable doctrinal details, have provided wisdom and ethical guidance to men and women in every era and culture and at every point along the IQ bell curve. If you're one who finds God talk troubling, all you need to muster, in order to benefit from Epictetus's advice here, is some level of appreciation for finding yourself alive in a cosmos you did not create and in which you are given, along with your share of trouble and strife, bountiful opportunities for wonder and joy. If Epictetus, a crippled former slave who lived under some of Imperial Rome's most treacherous rulers, found cause for, *and wisdom in*, adopting a fundamental position of humility and gratitude toward the universe, there is every chance that we, too, can benefit by embracing these attitudes.

Humility is a tricky subject, if only because it's impossible not to sound laughably pompous when recommending it. *Look here, you: Be humble!* But that's not it. We're not talking about personal humility of the kind that can be so treacherous if pursued head-on, the sort that easily warps into conspicuous, Uriah Heepish self-abasement that's the opposite of what it pretends to be. No, we're after a broader, more foundational humility, a mindset that grasps our status as utterly dependent beings and that has absorbed, fully, the fact of our mortality. We want a humility not of grovelling self-negation, but a clear-eyed recognition that every moment of our existence, as well as everything we have and are, is a gift. The mortality-humility connection is a natural one, and it is even reflected etymologically: Our word *humility* derives from the Latin *humus*, for soil or earth—that ground from which humankind arose, from which we draw our sustenance, and that will ultimately reclaim our bodies. We needn't take it to morbid lengths, but occasional reflection on life's contingency and brevity can provide a humbling perspective, one that can be both calming and a spur to greater engagement with life in the time left to us:

> 'Pass then through this tiny span of time in accordance with Nature, and come to your journey's end with a good grace, just as an olive falls when it is fully ripe, praising the earth that bore it and grateful to the tree that gave it growth.' Marcus Aurelius, *Meditations*, 4.48.

> 'Think of yourself as dead. You have lived your life. Now take what's left and live it properly.' Marcus Aurelius, *Meditations*, 7.56, trans. Gregory Hays.

Through humility then—the acceptance of life as an unearned gift—we arrive at gratitude. One of the simplest and most ready-to-hand balms for a muddled life is the age-old remedy of counting our blessings. Granted, life's bright spots can sometimes be hard to recognize, obscured as they often are by our day-to-day difficulties, by the usual dire headlines, and by the ongoing challenge of keeping our minds clear and our thinking straight. But when we can manage it, when the clouds part long enough to give us an objective glimpse of all we have to be thankful for, our gratitude can prove a strong antidote to the corrosive effects of cynicism, anger, sadness, and life's accruing jumble of petty disappointments. And by reminding us of the often-unrecognized abundance in our lives, it can help to temper the grasping acquisitiveness that sometimes seems to drive us, even against our will. Finally, as Epictetus suggests, gratitude can help us regain our lost sense of wonder.

This is not just Epictetus's idea. Gratitude is a virtue that enjoys high standing among the Stoics generally. Seneca, in *On Benefits*, says, "He who receives a benefit with gratitude repays the first installment on his debt." The first book of Marcus Aurelius's *Meditations* is a poignant and grateful accounting of his indebtedness to family, friends, teachers, and others. Cicero, in the *Pro Plancio*, called gratitude the greatest of the virtues, and "the mother of all the others". If you're like the rest of us, bringing gratitude to the fore in your life will likely require a conscious effort. If you regularly pray, meditate, or practise some form of reflection focussed on self-improvement, an easy step might be to add a minute or two explicitly to acknowledge those things, people, and events from your day for which you are particularly thankful. It's not difficult, and once you get started, the number of good things happening in your life, even within the space of a single unremarkable day, may surprise you; they will certainly encourage you. In addition to recalling specific moments—the pleasant encounter with the shop clerk, the encouraging email from a friend, the old car that started and ran smoothly despite the bad weather—you might also remember those broader circumstances of your life that apply, such as:

• a rational nature, a mind built for learning

- the presence, or the happy memory, of loved ones
- the ability, and the will, to rise above challenging circumstances
- good health
- meaningful work
- kindness from unexpected quarters
- a capacity for doing good
- nature: its power, beauty, and endless variety
- ...and so on.

Regular practice with this exercise can grow on you. If you're the journalling type, you can keep a written record of your reflections. You might even choose to follow the example of Marcus Aurelius (see book one of the *Meditations*) and write about the people in your life to whom you are most grateful for help in shaping your character, providing for your education, and encouraging your spiritual/philosophical growth. Keep these notes and reflections to yourself, though; blasting them out to the world via social networking can be a species of ego-stroking and will only sap their power. Marcus's *Meditations* were not written for publication; they were a tool for self-improvement and a form of spiritual exercise.

Once you're established on the gratitude wavelength, you can begin to notice its impact on your daily life—lengthening your patience, recalling your attention to life's smaller pleasures, and generally improving your resilience in challenging times. Humility and gratitude may or may not lead us to faith in God, but they can go a long way toward reawakening wonder and hope in even the most jaded adult.

HAPPINESS FOR SALE ~ WHAT WOULD SENECA SAY?

Laura Inman

On the front page of a section of *The New York Times* this weekend was an article about a psychologist who has studied happiness and has written a book on how to achieve it. The piece revealed very little of the author's secrets to happiness (I guess they might be called), but one observation of hers is that renters are happier than homeowners. Maybe that is indicative of other discoveries, like married people are happier or people in a certain region are happier. Maybe some people find that kind of thing interesting, like knowing somebody's astrological sign. However, as the path to happiness or as a way to live one's life, how could such conclusions have any validity or worth? Were the renters and homeowners in question so alike in all respects (even in most respects) with regard to happiness, save for their status as renters or homeowners, such that the difference in this *one* aspect could be the principal reason for one being happier than the others? Although the article was short on details on achieving happiness, perhaps so as not to pre-empt book sales, it did mention "hedonistic adaptation", which is the idea that we will eventually return, after experiencing joyful events, to a "base-line" emotional level, needing a new happy event to lift our spirits. It is not clear if the author pursues that idea to warn that seeking joy can actually run counter to happiness. Most absent was the suggestion on how to live happily when faced with genuine hardship or failure, those things that life generally has in store which undermine "happiness".

The ancient Stoics would not have thought that happiness could be gained from a set kind or number of external events; they conceived of "happiness" in a different way. For them, a key part of happiness was *tranquility*, that is to say a state of moderation, free from negative emotions. This approach might lack appeal to those who exalt in and strive for giddy highs, even though the painful emotional fall is inevitable; they see such a pendulum existence as 'really living'. The longer I live, and it has been quite a while now, the more I value emotional calm: I value it in others, I like the way it feels, and I work at obtaining it, although it does not come naturally to me. It is worth striving for that calm which John Keats rendered poetically in *Hyperion*:

'To bear all naked truths, / And to envisage circumstance, all calm, / That is the top of sovereignty. Mark well!'

Tranquility, for the Stoics, does not depend on renting or home owning, but on your internal qualities. Indeed, it depends, in my experience, on three key Stoic ideas. I set them out here, drawing on the thought of Seneca, so as to remind myself that happiness is not really 'for sale'.

The first is that we should *strive for mental self-sufficiency*. You have to be able to abide yourself, and use your own powers of rational thought to console yourself. As Arthur tells Bedevere at Camelot's demise in Tennyson's *Idylls of the King* (my paraphrase): "Comfort thyself, what comfort is in me, the old order changes and gives way to new and fortune fulfills itself in many ways." Also, the inner world is as valid as the external world. Read, study, exploit your talents and realize that, when it comes to accolades, few are enough, one is enough, none is enough. One quick glance at life and it is easily apparent that anyone who looks for happiness from external events is destined to be unhappy much of the time. Such a life is a version of a lottery game.

The second key principle is to *apply reason to emotion*. Reason is the one attribute that sets humans apart from the other animals; they have their special talents, and we have ours, reason. Use reason over emotion and understand that your feelings are not all-important, worth indulging, or determinative for yourself or others. Secondly, use reason to prevent yourself from thinking pointlessly, which is thinking about the aspects of situations over which you have no control. Instead, if you think you can act with effect, then do so, and when you know that you can't, stop occupying your mind with it; there is nothing more pointless than pointless thinking. Reason, formed from experience and logic, establishes that things can always be worse, what can happen to anybody can happen to you, and that death is life's neighbour; thus, realizing those things, you are at once appreciative of each peaceful moment and prepared for finding consolation in difficult times.

And, finally, we need *to understand what we are dealing with*. Adversity besets us all and creates us in large part, for better or worse. I don't have a lot of respect for, nor particularly like much, people who have not known adversity: How could anyone know what they are capable of, what they are truly like, when everything is nice and easy? We are at the mercy of fortune and all we have is on loan from fortune; our best efforts are worth doing, but will only take us so far. Reason will remind us that such is the lot of humanity and we share in common pain and suffering. If the moment at hand brings an opportunity for tranquility, take it; if not, try to find consolation within it. As Seneca said, "All life is bondage. Man must therefore, habituate himself to his condition, complain of it as little as possible, and grasp whatever of value is within his reach. No situation is so harsh that a dispassionate mind cannot find some consolation in it."

I am skeptical that buying a book on how to be happy will in any way lead to the desired outcome. A tranquil life is not achieved through a prescribed list of externalities; it may never be completely obtainable but, as the Stoics taught, we can make some real measure of improvement in our own existence by working toward tranquility through our own powers of reason.

References

Hadas M., *The Stoic Philosophy of Seneca: Essays and Letters*. W.W. Norton & Company, 1968.

SEE LIKE A STOIC: AN ANCIENT TECHNIQUE FOR MODERN CONSUMERS

Tim Rayner

Marcus Aurelius, the Stoic Emperor of the Roman Empire, grew up surrounded by beautiful things: great art and architecture, sumptuous foods, fine wines, and artfully tailored robes. By the time he became Emperor, he had everything that he could possibly desire. Marcus, however, was a Stoic philosopher, so he knew that *the law of life is change* and that one should never let oneself become too attached or invested in material things. To maintain his composure in the midst of plenty, he would seek to transform the way that he saw the things that he desired. This helped him get a grip on his desires and achieve peace of mind.

But Marcus's approach to consumables and other possessions also provides a handy guide for modern consumers who seek to overcome the allure of products that they want but don't need. Instead of looking at clothes, jewelry, food, and art through the lens of desire, Marcus advises that we view these things as pure material objects and evaluate them accordingly. He outlines this technique as follows:

'When we have meat before us and other food, we must say to ourselves: "This is the dead body of a fish, and this is the dead body of a bird or of a pig, and again, this Falernian [wine] is only a little grape juice, and this purple robe some sheep's wool died with the blood of a shellfish"...so that we see what kinds of things they are. This is how we should act throughout life: where there are things that seem worthy of great estimation, we ought to lay them bare and look at their worthlessness and strip them of all the words by which they are exalted. For the outward show (of things) is a wonderful perverter of reason, and when we are certain the things we are dealing with are worth the trouble, that is when it cheats us most.' *Meditations*, 6.13, trans. M. Hammond.

The best way to follow Marcus's approach in this passage is to turn it into a practical exercise. This is the approach that I take to philosophical concepts in *Life Changing: A Philosophical Guide*. The four steps to this exercise are:

Step One: Think of some item that you have coveted or continue to covet, such as an expensive house, a car, or some fashionable item of clothing or jewellery. Give this item a name and write it on a sheet of paper. This is your item of desire.

Step Two: Ask yourself: what is it that I find desirable about this item? Is it the look or design? The artistry that went into it? The social status that people attach to the item? The fragility or delicacy of it? The raw expression of power? Try to be honest about what attracts you about the item. Jot your answers down.

Step Three: Now apply Marcus's technique of material perception. Look at your item of desire and try describing it to yourself in strictly material terms. What stuff is it made of? Draw up a list of its material components. Forget about what you think of these components. Focus on the reality of the materials themselves. Are they soft, hard, squishy, rough? How do they sound when you scratch them with your nails? Are they common materials that are found everywhere, or rare materials derived from some far-off place? Note that the work that went into making the item, while a material process, is not a material feature of the item as such, and must be disregarded. Only the physical stuff that makes up the item should enter into your description of it.

Step Four: This brings us to the key step in the meditation. Try re-evaluating your item of desire seeing it as strictly material item. The goal here is to strip away everything glamorous and alluring about the item in question and to see it as a mere thing. Take some time to meditate on the object before you. Ask yourself, in light of these meditations, is it really as desirable as you'd thought?

Often we overestimate the value of things. Dazzled by their superficial allure, we mistake our impressions for the thing itself. Stripping items back to their material components – cotton, wood, glass, metal, stone, plastic, whatever – can help us get critical distance on our desire for these items. By stripping items back to their components, we are able to see through the glamour of things and understand them as the objects that they really are.

Doing this won't switch off your desire for material possessions. But if you dedicate yourself to practising Marcus's technique, you'll find that you can develop the resilience to resist these desires when they start becoming a problem for you. If nothing else, the meditation can help you get clear on precisely what it is that you value about the things you desire. Often what we desire about objects is not the thing itself, objectively speaking, but the social status that is associated with it. Other times what we see in objects is just our projection of value, or worse, someone else's attribution of value that we've unthinkingly come to accept. In the case of things like smartphones and computers, we often come to see that it's the functionality and connectivity that we desire, rather than the premium product itself. In the case of cars and fancy hotel rooms, we see that it's access to transport and accommodation that we desire, rather than an expensive vehicle in the driveway or a suite at the Ritz. For that reason, contemporary Stoics are collaborative consumers. They use ZipCar, a car sharing service, and AirBnB, a website on which people let a room, apartment or house.

Practising Marcus's Stoic technique sets you on a path of philosophical reflection that helps, over time, to reduce your desire for unnecessary possessions. So put yourself in training and have the courage to change your thinking: this is one of the ways you can aspire to a philosophical life of inner peace.

CONTROL YOUR EMOTIONS

Ryan Holiday

Would you have a great empire? Rule over yourself. PUBLIUS SYRUS

When America raced to send the first men into space, they trained the astronauts in one skill more than in any other: the art of *not* panicking.

When people panic, they make mistakes. They override systems. They disregard procedures, ignore rules. They deviate from the plan. They become unresponsive and stop thinking clearly. They just react—not to what they need to react to, but to the survival hormones that are coursing through their veins.

Welcome to the source of most of our problems down here on Earth. Everything is planned down to the letter, then something goes wrong and the first thing we do is trade in our plan for a good ol' emotional freak-out. Some of us almost crave sounding the alarm, because it's easier than dealing with whatever is staring us in the face.

At 150 miles above Earth in a spaceship smaller than a VW, this is death. Panic is suicide.

So panic has to be trained out. And it does not go easily.

Before the first launch, NASA re-created the fateful day for the astronauts over and over, step by step, hundreds of times—from what they'd have for breakfast to the ride to the airfield. Slowly, in a graded series of "exposures," the astronauts were introduced to every sight and sound of the experience of their firing into space. They did it so many times that it became as natural and familiar as breathing. They'd practice all the way through, holding nothing back but the liftoff itself, making sure to solve for every variable and remove all uncertainty.

Uncertainty and fear are relieved by authority. Training is authority. It's a release valve. With enough exposure, you can adapt out those perfectly ordinary, even innate, fears that are bred mostly from unfamiliarity. Fortunately, unfamiliarity is simple to fix (again, not easy), which makes it possible to increase our tolerance for stress and uncertainty.

John Glenn, the first American astronaut to orbit the earth, spent nearly a day in space still keeping his heart rate under a hundred beats per minute. That's a man not simply sitting *at* the controls but *in* control of his emotions. A man who had properly cultivated, what Tom Wolfe later called, "the Right Stuff."

But you . . . confront a client or a stranger on the street and your heart is liable to burst out of your chest; or you are called on to address a crowd and your stomach crashes through the floor.

It's time to realize that this is a luxury, an indulgence of our lesser self. In space, the difference between life and death lies in emotional regulation.

Hitting the wrong button, reading the instrument panels incorrectly, engaging a sequence too early—none of these could have been afforded on a successful Apollo mission— the consequences were too great.

Thus, the question for astronauts was not How skilled a pilot are you, but Can you keep an even strain? Can you fight the urge to panic and instead focus only on what you can change? On the task at hand?

Life is really no different. Obstacles make us emotional, but the only way we'll survive or overcome them is by keeping those emotions in check— if we can keep steady no matter what happens, no matter how much external events may fluctuate.

The Greeks had a word for this: *apatheia.*

It's the kind of calm equanimity that comes with the absence of irrational or extreme emotions. Not the loss of feeling altogether, just the loss of the harmful, unhelpful kind. Don't let the negativity in, don't let those emotions even get started. Just say: *No, thank you. I can't afford to panic.*

This is the skill that must be cultivated—freedom from disturbance and perturbation. So you can focus your energy exclusively on solving problems, rather than reacting to them.

A boss's urgent e-mail. An asshole at a bar. A call from the bank—your financing has been pulled. A knock at the door—there's been an accident.

As Gavin de Becker writes in *The Gift of Fear,* "When you worry, ask yourself, 'What am I choosing to not see right now?' What important things are you missing because you chose worry over introspection, alertness or wisdom?"

Another way of putting it: Does getting upset provide you with more options?

Sometimes it does. But in *this* instance? *No, I suppose not.*

Well, then.

If an emotion can't change the condition or the situation you're dealing with, it is likely an unhelpful emotion. Or, quite possibly, a destructive one.

But it's what I feel.

Right, no one said anything about not feeling it. No one said you can't ever cry. Forget "manliness." If you need to take a moment, by all means, go ahead. Real strength lies in the *control* or, as Nassim Taleb put it, the *domestication* of one's emotions, not in pretending they don't exist.

So go ahead, feel it. Just don't lie to yourself by conflating emoting about a problem and dealing with it. Because they are as different as sleeping and waking.

You can always remind yourself: *I am in control, not my emotions. I see what's really going on here. I'm not going to get excited or upset.*

We defeat emotions with logic, or at least that's the idea. Logic is questions and statements. With enough of them, we get to root causes (which are always easier to deal with).

We lost money. But aren't losses a pretty common part of business? Yes. Are these losses catastrophic? *Not necessarily. So this is not totally unexpected, is it? How could that be so bad? Why are you all worked up over something that is at least occasionally supposed to happen?*

Well . . . uhh . . . I . . .

And not only that, but you've dealt with worse situations than this. Wouldn't you be better off applying some of that resourcefulness rather than anger?

Try having that conversation with yourself and see how those extreme emotions hold up. They won't last long, trust that.

After all, you're probably not going to *die* from any of this.

It might help to say it over and over again whenever you feel the anxiety begin to come on: *I am not going to die from this. I am not going to die from this. I am not going to die from this.*

Or try Marcus's question:

Does what happened keep you from acting with justice, generosity, self-control, sanity, prudence, honesty, humility, straightforward-ness?

Nope. Then get back to work! Subconsciously, we should be constantly asking ourselves this question: *Do I need to freak out about this?* And the answer—like it is for astronauts, for soldiers, for doctors, and for so many other professionals—must be: *No, because I practiced for this situation and I can control myself.* Or, *No, because I caught myself and I'm able to realize that that doesn't add anything constructive.*

PART FOUR: LIFE STORIES

MY EXPERIENCES OF STOICISM

Helen Rudd

I. 2nd December, 2013.

I suffered a traumatic brain injury in May 2006.

Before my accident I was on the go all the time. I did aerobics every week, went swimming three times a week, sang in an opera group and a light operatic society, acted in plays and volunteered at the local theatre, and tried to walk everywhere. I had even run in the Hastings Half Marathon five times. At the age of 43, I had been an executive officer in the Inland Revenue for 21 years and one of my jobs had entailed being the manager of the local enquiry centre.

One day in 2006 I had just been swimming on my way to work when I was hit on the side of the head by a van, going probably at 30 mph, and rolled under a parked car. I was in a coma for three weeks, and then went to a brain injury rehab centre for a year, of which I remember nothing. Now my memory of anything about a year before the accident is fine but I remember nothing until about three years ago. I think it took me some time to realise fully what had happened to me. My Dad had to teach me how to read and write again, of which I had also remembered nothing. My symptoms now are: a slight loss of co-ordination, a loss of memory of about five years and a pretty bad loss of mobility. I don't use a wheelchair, I can walk outside as long as I have my stick and somebody is with me, and my balance is poor. I am medically retired from work.

My worst time was two to three years ago. I think that by then I had become fully aware of what had happened to me. I was extremely depressed to the point of not wanting 'to be' and I stayed in a local mental health resource centre twice. I stayed in bed all day and used to have screaming fits. If I had known what would happen a while ago I would never have believed it. I used to wonder 'Why me?'

At the start of 2013 I started to feel better psychologically, if not physically. This feeling of wellbeing has grown and now I am moving to a bungalow in the countryside tomorrow. I was listening to Radio 4 the other morning and heard about the *Stoicism Today* project. I realised then that Stoicism is what I'm employing now. I'm making the most of what life has dealt me, and I now think 'why *not* me?' I help people in ways that I'm still able, for example writing official letters, talking to people in a non-judgemental way who are suffering and not pretending I can help them if I can't, inviting friends round, which in turn helps me. I have become proud of the way I walk now in that I can't help smiling in spite of being unable to balance properly and I find that walking more slowly makes you look at things more, like walking around the lovely park here in the autumn with the shining golden trees and the dew on the grass. I have even passed an Open University module in psychology and intend to take a longer course in October.

The accident has given me a much fuller life. I have learnt things about the world, made friends with people I would never have even met before – and now when I see people jogging I feel glad that I don't have to do that because I can't. I honestly feel lucky that I survived the accident, met so many inspiring people and have learnt so much about life.

II. 19th January, 2014.

Just before I went down to Somerset with my Dad, I tried to think how a 'normal' person could employ Stoicism in order to feel happier and to gain a sense of achievement. I then remembered the feeling I had when singing in a concert with people who have Parkinson's disease earlier in 2013. It was the first concert I'd sung in since my accident, and halfway through I suddenly had an amazing feeling of: *yes, I love doing this, it is just where I want to be and I feel so proud to be singing with these really brave and friendly people.*

At the end of the year I found myself remembering this intense feeling, and I thought that the way to employ Stoicism is to think of how I **could** have felt and thought if I'd assumed a negative perspective. This could have included *why do I now have to sing with unwell people, why do I have to sing using words only instead of words and music which is what I was used to, nobody in this choir can read music like I can, I used to have Jane the conductor and soloist for singing lessons and I could be doing a much more highbrow concert than this...*

When I write these things now I feel horrible for expressing them, but it's a good example I think of realising that you can feel good about something that otherwise could be terrible. My plan would then be to notice how you feel about a situation, and then if it is positive think about how it could otherwise be negative and thereby know that you're employing Stoicism. Similarly, if you feel negative you could think about a positive way of looking at it and try to feel this new positive perspective.

I used this technique when travelling to Somerset in the car, and it worked! We go through Salisbury which is where Glenside is, the brain injury rehab centre where I lived for a year, even though I don't remember it. In the past I've had to close my eyes as we drove past it because it reminded me of what happened. So before getting to Salisbury I thought of how I'd be able to feel positive about it. My thoughts were that *I could think well, I used to be there but now I don't have to be, I'm coping in the outside world and it shows that I went to the best place for me.* So I deliberately kept my eyes open and asked my Dad to point the building out to me. I thought about these positive things and it was the first time I'd been able to look at Glenside 'in the flesh' as it were. I'm not saying it was easy, I can still remember how hard it was, but it worked.

Now as 2014 begins, I've adapted the way in which I've tried to think positively in everyday life. A few months ago I decided to note down three good things about the day just before I went to sleep, a contrast with the diary I kept 2 years previously about the bad things. As this has led me *automatically* to thinking about the good things, and not the bad, I decided yesterday that there's no need to do this any more. Instead, on December 31st each year, including this year, I'm going to write about happiness and why the year has been happy for me. I found it very rewarding to do this for 2013, a chance to take stock. Who knows, there may come a time when I feel there's no need even to do this.

I need to make the point that, in my case, I'm only able to do this now, some seven years after the accident. Before, I was in no fit state to employ Stoicism. I was too devastated by what had happened to me. There was a deep sense of shock and even disbelief. In the past year, however, I've discovered that I seem to be Stoic subconsciously.

So it *can* be done, even in terrible personal circumstances, provided the person concerned is ready.

III. May 25th, 2014.

I can honestly say that I feel better and better each week. My physical problems are still there but people have said my walking is more confident, and I'm sure that partly that is because of me not being embarrassed now about my wobbliness. I was telling a friend the other day about Stoicism and he said that what I'd told him had changed his view of the philosophy. He had always seen it as ignoring problems and just getting on with it, but now could see it's more about making the most of what you *can* do.

And my walking is a bit better since I moved into my bungalow in December. There is a lovely flat path in my back garden where I walk slowly and carefully back and forth for half an hour a day, no more, no less, without my stick. It is a gradual thing and some days are not as good as others. For example, yesterday I felt extremely wobbly and my legs wouldn't bend, but today was probably one of my best so far.

The walking practice gives me time to think, although I have to concentrate on the walking too. Basically what I've come to think is that Stoicism is all about making the most of your resources. It doesn't stop you feeling, say, hurt or anxious - for example, yesterday I wondered why I was not doing very well. But because I am in a more positive frame of mind now I just carried on with my day and concentrated on the here and now. As I did much better today I don't feel at all bad thinking about it, and this actually bears up my thoughts that you have to be in the right frame of mind to start trying to be Stoical. I realise that I've been acting in a Stoical way (such as listing the good things about my day, which I did for a while) that it's almost becoming second nature, if that's possible – I don't know!

I often look back on my 'black time' and think that if anyone had told me that in a couple of years' time I'd be doing what I do now I'd never have believed them. This includes things like getting up early, helping people fill in official forms, editing local newspapers for reading for the blind, cooking and baking cakes and, of course, learning and sharing people's experiences of Stoicism!

BEING A STOIC LAWYER

Paul Bryson

To take the common misconception of what it means to be 'Stoic', a 'Stoic Lawyer' would be some kind of emotionless, near robotic protector and relater of his client's goals. The same couldn't be said for me and I wouldn't want it to be. I'm a different kind of Stoic lawyer. Instead of striving to be a passionless automaton, I work to determine how the insights and teachings of the classical Stoic philosophers can improve me and my dealings, professionally and personally.

In explaining what it means to be a Stoic Lawyer, I shall focus in detail on the four qualities Zeno suggested the Stoic should cultivate:

- Wisdom, the knowledge of what is Good, Bad and Indifferent.
- Courage, the wisdom concerned with endurance.
- Temperance, the wisdom concerned with acquisition.
- Justice, the wisdom concerned with distribution.

I believe that each of these qualities has the power to improve me as a practising attorney in one way or another. As I strive to become a Wise, Courageous, Temperate, and Just lawyer, I believe I'll become a better lawyer.

Let's explore each aspect in more detail.

Wisdom

In distinguishing between what is Good, Bad, or Indifferent, I find it helpful to think of Epictetus's division of things between what is "up to us" and what is "not up to us". Arrian recorded that Epictetus said, "Some things are in our control and others not. Things in our control are opinion, pursuit, desire, aversion, and, in a word, whatever are our own actions. Things not in our control are body, property, reputation, command, and, in one word, whatever are not our own actions" (*Handbook*, §1). Notice that the first category of things are items where a person's exercise of the will can lead to virtue (or evil, which is the absence of virtue); the second category of things are all indifferent, in that they do not aid or harm the search for virtue because they are beyond the power of the will.

This influences my priorities. Reason dictates that I should spend my time focussing on taking the right approach to the first category. As it relates to my profession, the first category includes my composure, treatment of clients, opponents, employees, and third parties, how I maintain the confidences of clients, how I manage my office, and how I act to uphold duties of competence, loyalty, and diligence. By focussing on those things, instead of on things I cannot control, I believe I stand to gain not only virtue and tranquillity, but possibly a number of material "goods", such as the following:

- Juries will not be distracted by unprofessionalism.
- Opponents and third parties will be more receptive to my arguments and proposals.
- Clients will feel well-represented and will be more likely to pay on time and refrain from making disciplinary or malpractice complaints.
- I am more likely to develop a network of referral sources and colleagues who feel a genuine connection and respect for me.
- My reputation in the community will be that of a lawyer who does both well and good.
- As an additional benefit, I will not be driven into unprofessional conduct by seeking money or results at the expense of my professional integrity.

Courage

Initially, it is important to notice that Courage starts with Wisdom. That means that the focus remains, at least in part, on identifying and discriminating between the Good, the Bad, and the Indifferent. Courage is about applying Wisdom to areas of your life in which endurance is called for.

But what does endurance have to do with being a lawyer? The Classical Stoic writers frequently talked about a parade of horrors just around the corner—slavery, oppression by a murderous emperor, death by disease or violence. Most of those risks have been minimized by modernity; even illness, which remains part of the human condition, is less likely to result in death than it was in the days of Marcus Aurelius. But just like Marcus, modern lawyers are worried. They aren't worried about the Germanic tribesmen on the other side of the river, but about the student loan debt collectors who may call next week. They don't fear losing a limb or child to illness, but they dread losing their dreams of becoming the lawyer they went to law school to become. Either way, they share the emperor's feeling of powerlessness.

To summon their Courage, lawyers today need to remind themselves that the circumstances they face now or what they have done in the past cannot be changed. They can only affect the future. As for their present circumstances, lawyers should consider the limits of those circumstances. As Marcus noted, in *Meditations* 10.3, a person will either survive his circumstances or he will not. Stated another way: either a person will endure or she will not. To a Stoic, the mere fact of survival or death from those circumstances is indifferent for, ultimately, survival itself cannot always be within a person's control. The key is to remember to exercise Wisdom concerning those circumstances while they persist and concerning the course toward the future.

Courage impacts my practice by assisting me to carry on when things are difficult. I recently had a period of underemployment. Wisdom instructed me that underemployment was indifferent and temporary. Either I would find more opportunity, or I would perish (either physically or as a lawyer). I preferred to find more opportunity. So instead of sharing my bitterness at the opportunities that should have been given to me or blogging about how law school is a scam or suing my alma mater for failing to find me a job, I spent time networking, participating in *pro bono* clinics, and working in a non-lawyer capacity while developing plans for my next steps.

To me, that is the lesson of Courage. It is the wisdom to choose when to keep trying the same thing, when to try something else, or when to stop trying at all. It is also the wisdom to understand when the result is indifferent and when it is Good to keep trying anyway.

Temperance

Just as with Courage, Temperance begins with Wisdom. Instead of endurance, however, Temperance is Wisdom applied to matters of acquisition. For me, that focus on acquisition applies equally to the search for more and to the measurement of what I have already obtained.

As a lawyer, Temperance is important to me in a few different ways.

First, Temperance cautions me to pay attention to what it is I am seeking to acquire: is it Good, Bad, or Indifferent? Stoic teaching is that I should be spending time seeking the Good and avoiding the Bad, even at the expense of the indifferent. Wealth is one of those classically indifferent things, as is power. Stoicism influences me, therefore, to sacrifice the pursuit of wealth or power to pursue virtue, although it would be perfectly acceptable to have wealth or power if they were available. For that reason, money or influence is never a reason for using a strategy or methods that would lead me to abandon virtue, even for a moment. Temperance is a constant guard against that temptation.

Second, Temperance tells me to pay attention to whether what I have is enough. If it is, then there is no pressing need to seek more. As a lawyer, Temperance reminds me not to seek to represent more clients than I can handle or represent fairly. In turn, that helps assure that I can allocate the necessary time to represent the clients I have to the best of my abilities. By doing that, my reputation and referral base will naturally grow.

Justice

When I was in law school, an experienced lawyer remarked to me that lawyers are essentially in the business of moving resources from one column into another. On some level that is true of every practice area, assuming a broad enough definition of resources. Whether the resource is money, time, political/social influence, or something else, lawyers spend most of their time trying to cause a resource to flow in the direction of their clients or to prevent a resource from flowing away from their clients.

Justice is the use of wisdom about that distribution. In that sense, focussing on justice reminds me that the distribution of resources is often outside of my control. Although I have a duty to use my best efforts (both as a lawyer and as a Stoic), I have to face the reality that I don't control the outcome. I also have to face the reality that the outcome will rarely be something that makes my client believe that everyone is in the position he or she "deserves." Justice aids with this because it keeps me focussed on what is Good, Bad, and Indifferent concerning the distribution or redistribution of resources. By focussing on pursuing the Good, avoiding the Bad, and living with or without the Indifferent, I can better reconcile myself to the fact that there are days my clients lose when I think they should have won or win when I think they should have lost.

* * *

In conclusion, although Stoic thought is the key for me being happy in a stressful profession, I think what helps in general is having a philosophy of life. I have a framework through which I can interpret my universe and experiences and through which I can feel both control over the important portions of my life and satisfaction at my lack of control over other portions. By taking that philosophy seriously, even before I have all the answers or understanding, I have at least a strong mast to which I can lash myself securely against the tempests and siren calls of human experience.

THE STOIC MAYOR

Jules Evans

Introduction: Jules Evans writes about Sam Sullivan, mayor of Vancouver, Canada, from 2005 to 2008.

At the age of 19, Sam Sullivan, a lanky, athletic teenager from Vancouver, British Columbia, broke his spine in a skiing accident, and lost the use of his arms, legs and body. For six years, he battled with depression and suicidal impulses. Then he managed to get a philosophical perspective on what had happened to him, so that his spirit wouldn't be crushed along with his body. He says:

> 'I played many different mind games to get a perspective on what had happened to me – I don't mean games in a frivolous sense, but in the philosophical sense. For example, I imagined I was Job (the Old Testament prophet), and God was looking down on me and saying: "Anyone can manoeuvre through modern society with two good arms and two good legs, but let's take away the use of his arms, legs and body – now things are starting to get interesting, now let's see what the guy's made of".'

The young Sam displayed a typically Stoic approach to disaster, seeing adversity as an opportunity to test one's powers of agency and resilience. As Epictetus wrote:

> 'Difficulties are the things that show what men are. Henceforth, when some difficulty befalls you, remember that God, like a wrestling master, has matched

you with a rough young man. For what end? That you may become an Olympic victor, and that cannot be done without sweat.' *Discourses*, 1.24.

Sam's spiritual recovery from his injury involved a transformation from a passive victim of adversity to an active victor over it. He started to take control over the things he could take control over. He worked to regain the use of his biceps and interior deltoids. He contacted an engineering firm, and an engineer helped him devise technology, for example, to open the curtains, keep the freezer door open, cook TV dinners.

He says: "I could solve problems. When you're an able-bodied person, you don't really have a lot of focus. When you're disabled, you have to plan everything." He started to use his can-do energy to improve the life of others in the disabled community. He campaigned for better access for the disabled on Vancouver's streets, public transport and public services. He helped design sailing boats that could be used by the disabled, and campaigned for public funding for their introduction. He helped introduce disabled rock-climbing to Vancouver.

This sort of NGO activism gradually led him into local politics. He says: "I increasingly came up against the local government in my campaigning, and somebody I knew suggested I go into politics. So I did. In 1993, I successfully ran for a seat on Vancouver's City Council, running on the Non-Partisan Alliance (NPA) party ticket." Sullivan served on the Council for the next 12 years.

Then, in 2004, when his party sought a candidate for the 2005 mayoral elections, Sullivan's name was suggested – by that stage he was the party's only member of the City Council. He says: "I drew up a list of ten people who I thought would make a good mayor, and I went to them and asked them if they would run. They all turned it down, so I ran. And to my great surprise, I won."

One of his earliest international responsibilities as mayor of Vancouver was to travel to Turin for the closing ceremony of the 2006 Winter Olympics, and there to accept the Olympic flag from the mayor of Turin, in preparation for the 2010 Winter Olympics in Vancouver. He joked that it was strange Vancouver was sending the city's worst skier to the event.

Sullivan accepted the ten-foot Olympic flag and placed it in a special holder on his wheelchair, and then rotated his wheelchair to twirl the flag. He says he had practised the manoeuvre in car parks at night in Vancouver. The moment was seen by millions of viewers, and Sam was subsequently flooded with "around 5,000 emails, letters and phone calls, a lot of them from disabled people saying they had been inspired by the moment, though really, I don't consider accepting a flag as one of the great achievements of my mayoralty".

Sam says that part of the inspiration for his life of political activism comes from his admiration for the Stoics:

'One of the things that most attracts me to Stoicism is the commitment to public life, the engagement with society. Think of Zeno, hanging out on the painted porch, right in the centre of the action. Yet it also has the ascetic angle, the idea of detachment from worldly values. It's the idea you can fully engage with the world and still have that detachment running through your life. Stoics believe that is our duty to engage in politics, because politics is the fulfillment of our nature as humans and children of the Logos. Every human has a 'fragment' of the Logos within them – their rational soul – and this means that all humans are connected.

"We are all fellow citizens and share a common citizenship", Marcus wrote. "All are linked together by mutual dependence". One consequence of this belief is that Stoics believe it is our duty to put up with each other's foibles, as brothers and sisters put up with each other, and to work to try and help each other through public service, despite the foolishness of most humans, and despite the risks and sacrifices of public service.

If politics has improved, and become fairer and more civilised since the days of the Roman Empire, it is because good people have had the courage to go into politics, despite the risks, setbacks and vested interests they will inevitably encounter.'

He adds:

'Jumping into political life in the way that I did is a sacrifice, in a way. Politics is more depressing than it is exciting. For example, chairing public hearings, you encounter many people whose motivations often have little to do with the public good, and more to do with a private agenda. It can make one jaded, the type of demagoguery that goes on. If any honest person looks at it, there's not much critical thinking that happens there. There's a lot of bashing, a lot of 'gotcha' politics. It can be very hard for some to stomach.

The proper response to this kind of behaviour and environment is not to withdraw. It's to jump in, to try and put it on another vector. But you sometimes need to be Stoic not to be too depressed by what you encounter. I'd say to myself, "Well, not so long ago politics was run by intimidation and thuggery. At least there's a lot less blood spilt today". Because the Stoic tries to dedicate themselves to the common good, that means they don't merely work for their own supporters, their own tribe or electoral base, if they get into office. We hear from the historian Eutropius, for example, that Aurelius "dealt with everyone at Rome on equal terms".

You have government and you have politics. They require different values. In politics, you have to rigorously favour your friends and oppose your enemies, but in good government you have to be impartial, and try to rule for all society. Once you're in government, you should pursue government. I have a disdain for those who see government as merely an extension of politics – it's harmful to the public good. The Stoic tries to do what is right for the whole of society, rather than merely using government as a means to reward those who supported them. This idea, which perhaps seems obvious to us, was actually quite against the traditional Roman culture, which was rooted in the idea of debts, favours and family ties.'

In other words, the Stoic strives to do the right thing, rather than what's most popular. Sullivan says: 'There's a phrase of Marcus Aurelius' that I often think of – "the empty praise of public opinion". I don't think you can approach politics just to be popular. There's no point running for mayor just for the sake of being mayor. As Seneca put it, it's not how long you live but how nobly. Likewise, it's not how long you stay in power but what you do with it.'

He adds:

'I'm so not impressed with the judgment of public opinion. We've seen it be wrong so many times in history, at the most important times. That's why I got worried when I got high in the polls: it made me worry I was making really bad decisions. I'm more interested in the judgment of history – the judgment of intelligent people who have time to really consider what the issues were. The Stoic politicians of the past reminded themselves that politics was a grubby business run among people "whose principles are far different from your own", in the words of Aurelius. Politics was far more a duty than a pleasure for the Stoics, and if necessity forced one to leave the political stage, then one can leave gladly, and use one's newly-recovered leisure to concentrate on one's true love: philosophy. And indeed, many of the great classics of Stoic literature were written by people who were banished from the political stage. Their greatest philosophical achievements were born from political set-backs and failures.'

Sam Sullivan's time as mayor of Vancouver ended in 2008 when he was challenged for the leadership of the NPA party, and narrowly lost the vote.

He says: "My rival persuaded the party that it would lose the election heavily if I was the candidate. In the end, he lost the election heavily himself."

Sullivan muses: "I was the incumbent, and 80% of incumbent mayors are re-elected. So my party turned what should have been a comfortable victory into a rout." Does he resent his opponent for the damage he caused? "Sure, he damaged my political career, but I didn't mind that. In fact, I regularly toast him – he's the person who gave me back my freedom. Thanks to him, I can now do things like read books or go to the movies. I can make a commitment to do things with other people without making it contingent on there not being a crisis in the city. I actually prefer the contemplative life. Public service really is a sacrifice."

But he adds: 'What I disliked more was the repudiation of our political traditions – this was one person deciding his political ambitions would be the defining feature of the party. After I lost the leadership of the party, I tried to reason my way through. Many said they were going to quit the party. I convinced them not to. I said: "Suck it up, go into the election, and try to minimise the damage". It was clear the party was going to do badly, but I thought that if the public thought they'd seen a murder, it couldn't be a murder if they couldn't see a body. So I went out there and supported the new guy.'

He says:

> 'The one gift I could leave my party was modelling a new way of responding to adversity – a Stoic response. We've had models of leaders responding to perceived slights from their party, people who've let their party fall apart, or who have gone over to other parties. I tried to model a new response to adversity: when I get kicked in the teeth by my own people, I would suck it up, allow the criticism to go to me, and I would endorse the new guy.'

I ask Sam if he ever used his office to introduce Stoic policies to his city. He says: 'Stoicism is more about your actions and the way you live. It's not a religion that you could proselytise. I never really talked about philosophy as such. Vancouver is very much a cosmopolis, with a lot of different cultural groups living side by side, so you have to be respectful of people's different faiths and beliefs. Not that I read Epictetus or Marcus Aurelius every day. I just find great comfort in referring to them occasionally when things get rough.'

But, he adds:

'In some senses, my whole term was Stoic. For example, the Stoic idea of being a cosmopolitan was very useful to me. Vancouver is the most diverse, multicultural city in Canada, and quite possibly in the world. It's quite remarkable how many different ethnic communities we have. So that whole cosmopolitanism is very appropriate, certainly in Vancouver's context. Part of that led me to try to give respect to all the different communities. For example, I learnt some Cantonese in the election. Many people believe the reason I won was because of my facility in Cantonese. I was quite well supported by the Chinese-speaking citizens, the majority of whom are Cantonese. I also speak a bit of Mandarin, I learnt rudimentary words in Punjabi, I had some success in Italian, I can speak French, so the Stoic commitment to the cosmopolis is, to me, not at all out of line with being mayor of a city like Vancouver, and being a host to the world for the Olympics.

I also wanted the city to live according to nature. That was the whole idea of the EcoDensity project I set up – the idea that to make our cities environmentally sustainable in North America, we have to accept that we will need to live in high density cities, rather than sprawling suburbs. My view is that our present way of life, particularly the suburban culture, was running rampant over the environment. We're completely undisciplined in our approach to the way we live. I'd like to have a Stoic city, a city that's respectful of nature, that's conscious of its actions. Stoicism is the discipline of being able to understand the universe you're living in, and being more respectful towards it.'

THE GREATEST OF ALL STRUGGLES

Kevin Kennedy

'You will soon die, although you are not yet simple, not free from perturbations, nor without suspicion of being hurt by external things, nor kindly disposed towards all; nor do you yet place wisdom only in acting justly.' Marcus Aurelius, *Meditations*, 4.30.

Reading the above passage this morning, I felt as though someone had just given me a swift kick between the legs. Not that I expected to die anytime soon. (I'm 52: an advanced age in Marcus's day, but "the new 30" today.) Rather, I was wounded by the reminder that, despite all the years I had studied Stoic philosophy, I have still all too often allowed external events to disturb my peace of mind, behaved unkindly to those close to me, and failed to live according to reason and practical wisdom.

Aspiring to a Stoic lifestyle is easy, but only as long as we're never challenged to put our philosophy into practice. Such was the case throughout most of my adult life as I always lived alone or, if I happened to be living with someone else, still acted as though I were single. But then, late in life, I met a woman who I knew was "the one" and we had two children with each other. Suddenly my freedom had vanished, and I found myself facing responsibilities hitherto unknown to me. The greatest challenge was the task of staying home and taking care of our children on my own. As their mother has a regular job, and I – an eternal doctoral candidate, frustrated writer, and part-time tour-guide – only find myself working irregularly, I am charged with staying home with the children for weeks or even months at a time. Practicing Stoic *ataraxia* (serenity) and *prosoche* (mindfulness) is of tremendous help when trying to be a good parent. Acquiring these habits of mind requires daily training. Alas, there come the days when it becomes far too easy to cast all of my Stoic principles to the wind.

Yesterday was such a day.

I found myself alone with the children again. Their mother had left for work some hours earlier, leaving me with the task of maintaining some semblance of order in our home. But all I saw was chaos. The dishes were piled high in the sink, the laundry was all over the bathroom, the toys were lying out all over the place, and a large pool of urine was spreading over the parlour floor (my one-and-a-half-year-old son had run away from me before I could put a fresh nappy on him). Our home had become the site for a reenactment of the *Sack of Rome* by the Vandals. So, all in all, the perfect opportunity for me to practise Stoic virtues, to do what was in my power to restore order and not worry about the rest, to remember that my children were simply being children, and, no matter what happened, to treat them with kindness and care. But I forgot all that. Instead, I allowed the reptilian portion of brain to highjack my mind, and give free reign to my irrational impulses.

I screamed, as loud as I could. Nothing verbal, more a cry of desperation: AAAAAAGH. My son and my four-year-old daughter responded with stunned silence. There were no tears, only confused looks from small children trying to understand what their father had just done. I'll never forget the fear in their eyes, though. That was much worse than the sound of crying. Worse still was the realization that I had abandoned my philosophy. As Marcus Aurelius would have said, I was acting like a puppet on a string, allowing myself to be jerked around by irrational emotions. And then another passage from the *Meditations* came back to me:

'Let it be clear to you that the peace of green fields can always be yours, in this, that, or any other spot; and that nothing is any different here from what it would be either up in the hills, or down by the sea, or wherever else you will. You will find the same thought in Plato, where he speaks of living within the city walls "as though milking his flocks in a mountain sheepfold".' *Meditations*, 10.23.

I had to get back to that place of peace, but first I had to make amends. I apologized to my children, confessed to them that Papa had a little problem with his anger, and told them that, no matter what he said or did, he still loved them very much.

Only now do I finally understand Marcus, when he says that "the struggle against passion's mastery" is "the greatest of all struggles." But even Marcus himself struggled to achieve peace of mind. As the *Meditations* show, some mornings he didn't want to get up and go about his duties. He often thought the people he dealt with at court were cruel, duplicitous and stupid. Some days he had trouble controlling his desire for beautiful girls and boys. Moreover, he constantly had to remind himself to remain calm and to accept whatever Fate sent his way. If the emperor of Rome still managed to remain a decent human being, despite all of his travails, then how hard can it be for the rest of us today?

This morning I also read an obituary in an online newspaper. A cousin of mine, someone I had known well when I was very young, but hadn't seen in over twenty years, had died. He was 60. Only eight years older than I am. While I may hope not to follow him to the grave in the near future, my time, viewed from a cosmological perspective, still remains very short. Despite the moments when I fail to live up to the standards of Stoicism, I still believe that it is the best way for me to put whatever time I have left to good use.

THE STOIC DOCTOR

Roberto Sans-Boza

I recently developed an interest in Stoic philosophy as a very practical, logical and principled way of life. It has become important to me, both in my personal life and especially in my professional life. I work in a largely diagnostic specialty, and every day I have to confront severe diagnostic dilemmas. In this article, I reflect on how Stoicism has helped inform my medical practice.

As I started using Stoic philosophy, I tried to find some time each morning to plan my day and to reflect on certain philosophical principles. As I did this on the bus to work, I started to reflect on how little value I had put on my job as a way of becoming a better person. In particular, I asked myself this question: "What judgement would I pass on my medical career as a whole if today were the last day of my job?" In doing this, I realized that, rather than taking a big-picture view of how to be a "good doctor", I had focussed too much on the day-to-day experience of life, on the 'immediate' as it were. The overall purpose of what I was doing had become lost, obscured by all the details. From this, I also came to appreciate that one is not necessarily a good judge of oneself. Even though, through the last 20 years of my work, there was a clear pattern of professional expertise and dedication, my focus had nevertheless remained one of 'surviving' each day's challenges. In contrast, Stoicism led me to the realisation that I needed to find a more profound sense of inner satisfaction in my job instead of considering it just one of life's "necessary evils" in order to enjoy things that the pay-check can buy: material goods, holidays, books, and leisure time with family and friends.

There are four Stoic principles which have helped me especially in finding this inner satisfaction and purpose.

The first is that of 'mindfulness', the process of paying attention to the kind of thoughts I have from an ethical point of view. One of the ways I developed this was to imagine having a teacher or senior colleague, someone to whom I would aspire to be like myself, watching me over my shoulder when performing my duties. This approach led me to improve in all aspects of my professional life, starting with my competence and willingness to learn new techniques or to become updated in new procedures or treatments. I devoted a lot more time to study. Similarly, this approach has resulted in a strong sense of motivation to develop my teaching skills so I can become a more effective teacher.

The second key Stoic principle that I have found useful in my professional life is the idea that every person has a role to play and that my role, simply put, is *to help the patients as much as I can to recover their health*. I often think of this passage from Marcus Aurelius, in which he compares the different parts of the body working together for the good of the body as a whole with human beings working together for the common good:

> 'For we are made for co-operation, like feet, like hands, like eyelids, like the rows of the upper and lower teeth. To act against one another then is contrary to nature; and it is acting against one another to be vexed and to turn away.' *Meditations*, 2.1.

In my case, my role is to be as good a doctor as I can possibly be. This means putting aside irrelevant, often subconscious biases around unimportant things like the personal hygiene or unpleasant psychological traits of my patients, and always focussing instead on developing empathy with them, so as to help them better.

The third Stoic principle is the realisation that, in matters of disease, there are some things which are, sadly, beyond the possibility of intervention. As I mentioned at the start, every day I have to confront serious diagnostic dilemmas. In practice, this means that I often have to deliver bad news to patients on a daily basis, in those cases where the tests I perform confirm the presence of severe, painful or irreversible conditions. This is not an easy thing to do. Indeed, I used to feel an increasing sense of frustration that I could not help those particular patients and this, in turn, led to bouts of sadness and desperation. Adopting a Stoic attitude, however, has led me to focus on what I *can* do, and that is to perform the diagnostic tests as accurately as possible so as to minimize suffering, and to continue to study more so as to improve my diagnostic skills. When I share negative results with my patients, I now try to do so in a way which emphathizes fully with their suffering, but also with a certain detachment which, crucially, allows me to *carry on*, and not be dominated by feelings of sadness or guilt.

The fourth helpful Stoic idea is the realisation that we are a minuscule particle in the vastness of space and time. In this frame of reference, sufferings related to social status, personal victories and settling of scores with colleagues or administrators have lost much of their importance. This realisation has encouraged me to focus more on what is *actually* important: to play my part in the great theatre of life, and do that well. Thus, when my time comes, I will be able to be grateful and happy to have been a useful part of the cosmos in which we managed to exist. My enjoyment of daily life has been greater and my tolerance of unpleasant or hostile co-workers or managers has improved, so I can get much more out of my job, which has become again a source of personal, intimate satisfaction, and even more so when it is hard or unpleasant.

All in all, reflecting on Stoic ideas and principles like these has led to the personal admission that that most of my favourite fantasies in the past were linked to the idea of retiring early and returning home. I used to hope that, once there, I would live a "care–free" existence, liberated from the daily burden of being surrounded by suffering and giving bad news. I have now realised how vain these idle thoughts were. Of course, I must prepare for retirement as part of the natural cycle of life, but I am now intent on finding enjoyment and satisfaction in my present personal circumstances, finding meaning in doing my job well and becoming a better doctor every day.

I often think of the many colleagues who, in increasingly alarming numbers, admit to being tired of and disillusioned with the practice of medicine. This profession has become more and more scientifically complex, more and more alienating as the freedoms that we used to enjoy in our decisions are increasingly curtailed by the limitations imposed on us by managers, restrictive budgets and political decisions. I think that the public good is damaged by the loss of excellent, caring and dedicated professionals who quit in order to find peace or fulfillment doing other things, or just doing nothing. The Stoic ideals might be useful to find satisfaction in our careers, mostly by understanding what it is that cannot be changed by us individually, but also through leading by example and reflecting on our public duty to our fellow human beings. We have been given the privilege of doing one of the most exciting jobs that one can have, and it is unlikely that we will be equally useful to society in other occupations. Even if we do not need or seek monetary or social recognitions, it is difficult for me personally to imagine a better way to have spent my limited time which is, of course, the only *real* possession we have.

MUSINGS OF A STOIC WOMAN

Pamela Daw

I. The Tyranny of the Urgent

The following passage was my Stoic reading this morning:

'O mortals, where are you hurrying to? What are you concerned with? Why do you go this way and that, miserable, like blind men? You are going the wrong way, and have forsaken what is right. You seek prosperity and happiness in the wrong place, where it is not; nor do you give credit to another who shows you where it actually is. Why do you seek it from externals? For it is not in the body...it is not in wealth: if you do not believe me, look at Croesus, look upon the rich of the present age, how full of lamentation their life is. Happiness is not in their power; for, otherwise, those who have been consuls two or three times must be happy, but they are not.' Epictetus, *Discourses*, 3.22.3.

My immediate thoughts in response were: 'The Tyranny of the urgent... our world moves at such a rapid pace. We fill our days in the pursuit of so many things that have no intrinsic value in the grand scheme of our lives. How many of us are ill from a lack of time spent in healthy pursuits? How many of us now reap the crop of the seeds that we planted in our past? Let us be ever mindful of our actions and the consequences that come from those actions. Let us take the time to care for our bodies, and to nurture our souls to the best of our abilities. To pursue the "big rocks" in our lives and not to get bogged down by the daily minutiae. To live in the present without regret from the past or fear of the future. To live a flourishing life, filled with joy and steadfastness.'

As a wife, mother, daughter, sister, business owner, friend and all of the various roles that I have in this life, what are my big rocks? The largest rock in my life would be my amazing husband, Michel Daw, my rock of Gibraltar. My first rock, therefore, is him and to continue to nurture our relationship. My next rock would be my children, to be able to make time to continue to see them and spend quality time together even though they are grown-up with their own households and careers.

The next big rock is my relationship with my mother who has been ill lately, and is coming to the end of her life. A huge priority in my life right now is to spend as much time as possible with her while she is still able to have conversations, to let her know, as always, that she is loved and has so much value to me. To let her know that, no matter what adventure may await us after death, she will continue on in my memories of her. I am focussing on enjoying sitting with her in quiet moments, looking at photographs, talking of the past, nesting with her in her illness. Trying to squeeze as much juice out of the fruit of her life while she is still with us.

In focussing on spending time with my Mum, I then come to the big rock of my sisters. They are the ones who are bearing the weight of caring for an aging parent. I am the one who lives four hours away from my mother while they are all within a fifteen-minute drive, and one actually lives in the same home. They are the ones who are struggling with the daily requirements while trying to balance their own big rocks of marriage, family and health. It is important for me to take the time now to try to relieve some of their burdens, to continue to nurture my relationship with them. To keep the lines of communication open so that they have someone to talk to when the darkness of illness begins to envelop their own lights. To be an ear to vent to when everything just feels like it is too much to bear.

My next big rocks are smaller in size but are still big enough to need to go into the jar next: my business and my friends. Working from home there is often the challenge of time bleeding away with the 'tyranny of the urgent'. I am starting to enforce the practice of setting "business hours" so that I can be more productive with my time and more focussed when I am working. My friends are the rock that is very hard to fit into the jar at the moment with the increased need to travel and visit my mother. Many of our friends are also involved in the Stoic workshop sessions that we hold in our home on a monthly basis. This means that they are wrapped into the bedrock of my life, Stoicism. Stoicism is what my jar is made of. It is not glass, but rather strong and made of fired obsidian.

What does Stoicism bring to my life in practice?

- living consciously (planning with reservation, knowing that things can change with a moment's notice)
- stewardship (my body is the only one that I get, my home)
- mindfulness of our planet (trying to live with as small a footprint as possible, conscious of our place in the universe)
- virtues (trying to live with the virtues as my guidepost, doing the right thing because it *is* the right thing)
- letting go (knowing what is in my control and what is not)
- relationship (my place in the world and the importance of those around me)

Now that my big rocks are covered I know that I have very little time for the minutiae that come into my life. I have lately found that some pursuits that I find less fruitful, such as spending too much time on Facebook or watching television, have been pushing for prominence in my life at the expense of others. Maybe this has been a coping mechanism for my mind to process the news of my mother's ill health and imminent passing?

I am going to continue to work on achieving balance in my life, ensuring that my big rocks do not get crowded out by Facebook or the television sand. In other words, my aim is to ensure that "authenticity" continues to be the main goal of my stay while visiting this planet.

II. At the Journey's End

'How do we act in a voyage? What is in my power? To choose the pilot, the sailors, the day, the time of day. Afterwards comes a storm. What have I to care for? My part is performed. The subject belongs to another, to the pilot. But the ship is sinking: what then have I to do? That which alone I can do; I am drowned, without fear, without clamour, or accusing God; but as one who knows that what is born must likewise die. For I am not eternity, but a man: a part of the whole, as an hour is of the day. I must come like an hour, and like an hour must pass away. What signifies it whether by drowning or by a fever? For, in some way or other, pass I must.' Epictetus, *Discourses*, 2.5.2.

My response to this was: "Have courage to face the inevitable with reason and peace. Do what you can to influence or change your circumstances, but when you have done all that you can, act with dignity."

I have recently experienced a momentous loss in my own personal life. My mother passed away from a terminal form of cancer within four months of diagnosis. The example that my mother gave me of "grace under extreme adversity", "peace when the storm of life is raging", will stay with me for the rest of my life and with anyone who witnessed her incredible dignity and fortitude. Upon her initial diagnosis she spoke with her doctors and specialists, discovered that there was little medical intervention that would prolong her life considerably, and made the choice to accept the inevitable and to spend what little time she had left with family and friends around her. She chose not to rail at the circumstances or to fight the inevitability of death, but to accept things with serenity. Her moments, although tinged with regret that she would not experience the future with those that she loved, were filled with important words, love and friendship.

I am blessed to have been part of her final days, blessed to have had such a mother. I am blessed to have known such a woman, an example of dignity and virtue in the face of insurmountable and unbeatable adversity.

When we are given a circumstance or challenge in life, we must first examine our future actions virtuously. Secondly, we must act as we have determined virtue would demand, and then we must accept the outcome, understanding that we have done all that we could. We can then let go and move forward into the sea of life, able to release the outcome and enjoy the journey.

OF SKUNKS, SAUERKRAUT AND STOICISM

Erik Knutzen and Kelly Coyne

We are "urban homesteaders" — that is to say, low-tech, low-rent Martha Stewarts. Urban homesteading is a DIY, self-reliance movement consisting of a wide constellation of activities, from edible gardening to home brewing, from keeping chickens to bread baking, from frugal living to community building. It's an eminently practical lifestyle.

That practicality is why Stoicism works so well as the philosophical operating system of urban homesteading. While Foucault and Hegel might help me navigate the epistemological frontier, when I'm staring at a carefully tended vegetable bed that just got destroyed by a skunk, you can bet I'll reach for Seneca.

When you spend much of your time, as we do, rummaging around on the Island of Forgotten Skills, trying to teach yourself crafts long forgotten by your grandparents, you're certain to run into setbacks, frustrations, and plenty of outright failures. The skunks are, so to speak, everywhere.

These challenges, however, are more valuable than the activities themselves. Take Seneca's horticulturally sound and psychologically wise advice:

‘No tree becomes rooted and sturdy unless many a wind assails it. For by its very tossing it tightens its grip and plants its roots more securely - the fragile trees are those that have grown in a sunny valley. It is, therefore, to the advantage even of good men, to the end that they may be unafraid, to live constantly amidst alarms and to bear with patience the happenings which are ills only to him who ill supports them.' *On Providence*, §4.

How do you learn to "live constantly amidst alarms?" For practice, try commuting by bicycle in Los Angeles. It took years of riding for me to become accustomed to riding alongside impatient, often distracted motorists. A Stoic would argue that: "Anger, if not restrained, is frequently more hurtful to us than the injury that provokes it." Odds are that if I turn to give a finger to a misbehaving motorist behind me, I'll only run smack into the one drifting into my lane ahead of me.

Do I still occasionally get angry while riding? Of course. Stoicism is a path, not a destination. Achieving the tranquillity of mind of a great Stoic master takes a lifetime. But at least I'm trying. More important, perhaps, than getting some exercise and avoiding fossil fuels, riding a bike in traffic is an exercise in the acquisition of tranquillity of mind.

To step out into the garden, to forage edible weeds in the woods, to cook from scratch or ride your bike means closing your Facebook timeline and the endless text messages on your phone. It means saying goodbye to the news of crack smoking mayors and twerking celebrities. To inhabit the contemporary mediasphere is to live a life, as Cleanthes' oft-quoted maxim goes, "...like a dog tied to a cart, and compelled to go wherever it goes." When we let the cart pull us we lose our free will. We lose the very things that can really change the world: the small, sincere efforts of hand and heart.

Instead of running behind the cart, we can gather the ones we love, our friends neighbours and community, to work on the things we can change and not worry about that which we cannot. Urban homesteading gives us all a chance to make a difference, to transform the world one bike trip, one lush garden, one homegrown apple, one crock of sauerkraut at a time.

PART FIVE: STOICISM FOR PARENTS AND TEACHERS

STOICISM FOR COPING WITH TODDLERS

Chris Lowe

My fall into parenting, though planned, came rather abruptly when our twin boys arrived 12 weeks early. Even then, years before I discovered Stoicism, we handled some stressful times quite stoically. Eleven weeks of feeding tubes, monitors and transfusions could have been incredibly stressful, but we managed to take it one day at a time and keep a rational mind.

My fall into Stoicism, by contrast, has been far more gradual. I stumbled upon Stoicism from a finance blog. I read *A Guide to the Good Life* by William Irvine, started a blog and participated in Stoic Week 2013.

As our kids have grown to be three years old my own flaws have become ever more apparent, mirrored back to me by the reflective-sponges that are my kids. This reflection of myself has definitely pushed me to better myself. It's through Stoicism that I seem to have found ways to improve myself and my kids.

Raising good, productive members of society is one of my primary duties as a parent. As parents, we must teach and appropriately model for our children. If we don't actually make a mess of our kids, and instead raise them with good manners, discipline, values and a work ethic, then they could actually spread more good in this world. I believe Stoicism has a lot of the tools needed to raise children well: children who will understand their emotions, be conscientious and respectful of others, have a strong work ethic and be resilient and flexible to changes throughout their lives. Trying to apply that to our children, my wife and I try to be mindful of the behaviour of our kids, their personality traits and characteristics. She comes from a special education and applied behavioural analysis background. This scientific / empirical element to our parenting, combined with influences from a Montessori education and our unique family backgrounds, has seemed to encourage a couple of great kids. Our parenting approach so far is to foster the positive traits and skills and to discourage, by ignoring, the traits and behaviours we judge as negative. If by teaching our children appropriate skills for coping, they have a greater chance of flourishing as adults and of contributing positively to society, then we will have accomplished our duty as parents.

A Stoic analogy I have found particularly helpful is that of an archer drawing his bow. You can train and develop mastery of the skill, but once you release the bow you can't control the flight of the arrow. Winds or other influences may change its course and we must be prepared to accept that. It is the teaching and modelling we do for our kids that prepares them for the future; but our preparation only carries them so far and the rest is out of our control. Reminding myself of the dichotomy of control has been one of the more practical applications of Stoicism I have found. For example, the behaviour of my kids, in the past and in the current moment, is out of my control. I do, however, have control over how I approach teaching them, hopefully impacting their future behaviour. It is my duty to teach my children to react properly to disappointment and to be resilient.

I've reached the conclusion that toddlers are simply impulsive creatures, bent on satisfying the desire of the moment. Unenlightened Hedonists. They don't yet know any better and lack full rationalization skills to delay gratification or understand the context of their actions. How they react to their desires not being fulfilled depends on how my wife and I raise them.

Toddlers testing their limits, exercising power and throwing tantrums, are all part of a toddler living in accordance with their nature. To desire, or expect, otherwise would be foolish and certainly placing your happiness at the disposal of forces outside your control. The difficulty in correcting behaviours is identifying which are developmentally appropriate, or in accordance with nature, and which are inappropriate, or detrimental to the child's flourishing.

In my limited experience, most inappropriate behaviours are learned. Patterns and routine, such as allowing your kids to watch TV while you cook, may form rules in a child's mind, resulting in a meltdown when the routine inevitably breaks. By responding to and coddling a crying child you are reinforcing their concept that crying solves problems. We focus on telling our kids that they need to use words to talk and communicate, trying strictly to ignore behaviours like tantrums and whining.

With one of the boys we've noticed flexibility issues around the order of operations. Occasionally he has had a tantrum because I pulled him out of the car and carried him inside, when he had actually wanted to do it himself. He would not end his tantrum until I had carried him back to the car to start all over. So, for a while we made an effort to keep things a bit random and ignore the tantrums until he learned some flexibility. The hope is that we build his resilience to stressors in life therefore becoming more prepared for the future.

I can only hope that I have prepared myself and my children the best I can to contribute positively to society. I don't want to nurture super-kids necessarily, who are master violinists or can speak 6 languages. Though those skills would be great, they are not necessary, and in my opinion, focus on the wrong priorities. I want to raise children that are critical thinkers, creative, kind and generous: people who leave the world better when they leave than when they arrived.

I'm a better parent in theory than in practice. I'm often slipping and missing my step and I have moments when I'm not mindful and I react wrongly and do more damage. I try to recognize and remember those shortfalls, forgive myself and correct them for the future. My goal is to become more mindful and to become a better parent, husband and person.

FATHERHOOD AND STOIC ACCEPTANCE

Jan Fredrik-Braseth

Despite having studied philosophy for several years, I discovered Stoicism just a few months ago. My first meeting with Stoicism was through the participation in Stoic Week 2013. I was immediately inspired by the thoughts of the ancient Stoics, and I found that I was in agreement with many of their ideas on how to live a happy life.

A couple of months before Stoic Week, I became a father for the first time. It turned my life upside down. I have always been very active and have several interests that I like to spend time on. Even when I did not have a full-time job, the day was not long enough for me to do everything I wanted. Having a child forced me to make some major changes about how I was living my life. Suddenly, I had to spend almost all my spare time taking care of my son, and this was really hard for me to handle.

I was the most frustrated when I tried to make him go to sleep. My son was not (and still is not) a very good sleeper. It could take more than an hour of hard work to get him to sleep. During that time I had to carry him around, or else he would cry. I remember thinking things like: "Why can you not just go to sleep? I do not have time for this! I want to be able to do such-and-such!" The same thoughts arose when doing other necessary activities with him. It was not that I did not want to spend time with my son, but I also wanted to spend time on a bunch of other things, and those two did not go together.

Learning about Stoicism made me realize that I could apply Stoic teachings to handle this new situation better. The three principles which inspired me the most are the following (these are my paraphrases and interpretations of what the Stoics said):

1. You should not spend time worrying about things you cannot control.
2. The most important thing in life is to live virtuously.
3. You should try to excel at any role you may have.

As the regards the first, it was very clear that there were several things in this situation that were out of my control. I *did* have a son I had to take care of. I could *not* control how much he slept, or when he went to sleep or woke up. I *did* have less time for doing things for myself. None of these things were in my control, and it makes sense that I was only making myself unhappy by thinking about how "unfair" they were, or how I wished things were different.

I also quickly noticed a virtue which I found the need to practise, and which I get ample time to practise nowadays: *patience*. Every time my son spends an extra long time going to sleep and I start thinking about all the other things I want to do, I remind myself that this is a perfect time to practise patience. I am actually pretty patient in a lot of situations, and I consider this a very good quality to have, therefore I am grateful that I get to practise it even more. I think this demonstrates what Epictetus meant when he said: "Seek not for events to happen as you wish but rather wish for events to happen as they do and your life will go smoothly" (*Handbook* §1.8). Rather than wishing to be somewhere else, I am grateful to be in such a situation, because I can practise cultivating virtue.

I was also inspired by the Stoic idea of excelling in any role you may have. I started thinking about how a perfect father would be, and it became clear to me that a perfect father should be there for his son when he needs him, and he should not complain about having to spend too much time with him. Thinking about this made me realize the meaningfulness of raising a child, and made it easier to wake up in the middle of the night and walk around holding him for an hour.

My son has grown older, and is now sleeping a little better. On the other hand there are other things to do with him that now take more time. I cannot say I never think about what other things I could spend my time on, but I certainly enjoy my role as a father a lot more than a few months ago. I still have to remind myself that patience is a virtue I like to practise, and that there are no good reasons for complaining about things you cannot control.

However, nowadays I can often enjoy just sitting still, waiting for my son to go to sleep.

PRAISE THE PROCESS

Matt Van Natta

There is a growing body of evidence that praising children for attributes like intelligence or athletic ability backfires as a means of promoting achievement. Well meant praise can often send a message to a child that certain aspects of their life are fixed ("I'm smart at this, but I'm dumb at that"), as argued in a recent article by Katrina Schwartz. If a child internalizes the belief that they are either naturally good at something or not, it undermines the determination that is necessary to learn, grow, and eventually master a skill. Thankfully, Stoicism offers a perspective and some exercises that complement these findings so that our own children avoid the pitfalls of such a poor perspective.

* * *

'It's really about *praising the process they engage in*, not how smart they are or how good they are at it, but taking on difficulty, trying many different strategies, sticking to it and achieving over time.' Carol Dweck, Professor of Psychology, Stanford.

Professor Dweck's research shows that praise should be directed at the process of learning, rather than focussed on the outcome. In other words, pat your child on the back for engagement with a subject and encourage their efforts to avoid frustration as they run into, then overcome, obstacles. Remind them that failure is a part of learning and then help them devise new strategies for success. Don't simply proclaim, "You got the right answer, good job!" and definitely don't say, "You're such a smart kid!" and call it a day.

Historically, Stoicism has frowned upon praising people in the way that Carol Dweck advises against, in that Stoics didn't generally say: "You're really great at X!" either. For instance, here is Epictetus's definition of a person 'succeeding' at Stoicism:

'The marks of the proficient person are that he censures no one, *praises no one*, blames no one, accuses no one, says nothing concerning himself as being anybody, or knowing anything. When he is, in any instance, hindered or restrained, he accuses himself, and, *if he is praised, he secretly laughs at the person who praises him* and, if he is censured, he makes no defense.' *The Handbook, §48*

To the ancient Stoics, praise had no utility. Marcus Aurelius put it this way:

'Everything which is in any way beautiful is beautiful in itself, and terminates in itself, not having praise as part of itself…What is beautiful because it is praised, or spoiled by being blamed?' *Meditations*, 4.20.

Of course, in the Roman court the praises Marcus overheard were not only useless, from a philosophical point of view, but they were also manipulative. Praise was political, meant to sway people one way or the other. Parental praise, we can hope, is at least meant well but as we've seen, praise of the wrong type can be damaging.

In contrast, the 'Praise the Process' perspective, which Carol Dweck recommends, actually fits easily within the Stoic framework. In *Meditations* 10.33, Marcus Aurelius makes a rare positive comment concerning praise,

"...a man becomes both better, if one may say so, and more worthy of praise by making the right use of these accidents." The "accidents" Marcus mentions are the misfortunes of life. What is the Emperor willing to praise? A person's ability to respond well to circumstances. He won't congratulate you on your 'natural' intelligence, strength, or beauty, but he will applaud your wise actions. Wisdom, for Stoics, is not an internal trait of which you have a set amount, but is rather the manner in which you approach the circumstances of life. Wisdom is the process of living well: the most important thing is *how* you go about things. It's worth praising that process.

* * *

So, outside of praising the process, what specific Stoic exercises can we, as parents, use with our children to build some grit and determination into their perspectives? Consider this:

> 'Allow not sleep to close your wearied eyes, until you have reckoned up each daytime deed: "Where did I go wrong? What did I do? And what duty's left undone?" From first to last review your acts and then reprove yourself for wretched (or cowardly) acts, but rejoice in those done well.' Epictetus, *Discourses*, 3.10.2-3.

The above quotation supports a Stoic practice called the 'Evening Reflection'. Many of us go through this process nightly before bed. I'd like to suggest bringing this meditation to the family dinner table.

The Evening Meditation consists of reviewing three questions: "What did I do today? What did I do amiss? What was left undone?" Professor Dweck believes that "...families should sit around the dinner table discussing the day's struggles and new strategies for attacking the problem. In life no one can be perfect, and learning to view little failures as learning experiences, or opportunities to grow could be the most valuable lesson of all." As Stoic parents, we can practise this idea and grow in our philosophy while doing so. I suggest that as we gather our family around a meal, where we probably already ask, "What did you do today?" we add the questions: "What did you succeed at and struggle with today?" and "What needs to be done tomorrow?" We can share in the triumphs of our children's day. We can share our own challenges so that our children understand that struggle is to be expected. We can plan together, as a family, our strategies to overcome obstacles big and small. In doing so, we build an understanding of, and appreciation for, the process of learning in our children (and ourselves) and they will be all the stronger for it.

Praise matters. Children need feedback to help them understand the world around them. But research shows that it is how we praise others that is important. Like the ancient Stoics, we can choose to praise those things that lead to wisdom and, in doing so, we will help our children thrive.

References
Schwartz, K., 'Giving Good Praise to Girls: What Messages Stick': http://blogs.kqed.org/mindshift/2013/04/giving-good-praise-to-girls-what-messages-stick/

STOIC TEACHING AND STOIC CONTROL

Michael Burton

The Stoic notion of control is the idea that essentially in life there are three types of events that can befall an individual: those that are completely under one's control, those over which one has some but not complete control, and finally those over which one has no control. The Stoics advise us that the key to tranquility lies in being able to identify which of these events face us in our day-to-day lives and more importantly, only to concern ourselves with the first and second type of events. In applying the Stoic notion of control to teaching, I will argue that educators can benefit from a deeper understanding of what they can control (i.e., how they teach), those things that they have some but not complete control over (student learning itself) and what is out of their control (student *attitudes* towards learning),

Let's start with the last of these, the fact that one must first acknowledge and accept that there are some things that are out of our control. First and foremost, the teacher has no control over the attitude a student may take towards their learning. Coming into your classroom, a pupil has had years to decide how they feel about learning, and sometimes these attitudes are quite negative. Certainly, you can hope that your approach to teaching might make such students change their attitude, but you should not depend on it as this does not fall within the scope of your control. You cannot impact another individual's thoughts, attitudes, or emotions if they are not willing to hear what you have to say. Ideally, learning is a reciprocal process which, in order to be successful, must comprise of both a willing teacher and student. You will have limited success trying to teach anything to a student who does not see any value in learning.

But, by acknowledging the idea that students' attitudes are not something in the scope of the teacher's control, teachers can begin instead to ask the right types of questions, and plan the right kinds of lessons, in order to bring about better learning outcomes for their students. This is something teachers *do* have complete control over. The key thing is to approach students with lessons and ideas that are not only going to interest them, but that will also show *intrinsic value*. Indeed, every teacher must believe, and convey with passion, that what they are teaching is essential to the individual growth of the students in front of them. This is how learning becomes contagious. While we cannot control what our students' attitudes are towards learning, we can control *what* we teach and *how* it is taught. With the right approach and a clear sense of passion, we can hope that our students will change their attitudes and see the value in their education.

Despite this, at times even a highly motivated, interesting, and passionate teacher, who can demonstrate the intrinsic value of learning to students, can fail. Similarly, any teacher who believes that they are able to meet the educational needs of every student who walks into their classroom is naive. It is simply not possible to teach effectively every student whom you encounter in your teaching career. Unfortunately, there are going to be some pupils who, despite your best efforts, will see no value in what you are trying to do. You could take this information and say, like many outside of the classroom do, that you have failed as a teacher - but is this really the case?

Ultimately, teaching is analogous to a doctor treating a patient. The doctor can recommend the best course of treatment for a patient and do everything by the book, but if the patient sees no value in the doctor's advice and continues to live in opposition to his recommendations, can we really hold that doctor responsible for the poor health of his patient? You can bring all the passion and enthusiasm you want into the classroom but unfortunately, with some students, you will fail to convince them that what you are doing is worthwhile. In the end, the choice to learn resides with the student, not the teacher, just as the choice to live a healthy lifestyle lies with the patient and not the doctor. Unfortunately, many of the students we face are unaware that their decisions not to pay attention or see the value in their education can have long lasting effects on their lives. But this is a problem inherent within the educational system that is beyond the scope of this article to address.

In conclusion, teachers have no control over students' attitudes towards learning, some but not complete control over student learning itself, and complete control over what we teach and how we teach it. Realizing this can relieve some of the stress teachers feel when it comes to engaging every student they stand in front of. Importantly, this need not rid the educator of their professional responsibility and accountability. It simply shifts our focus as teachers to that which we can control: putting our best foot forward to convey our passion, enthusiasm, and knowledge about our subject, trying our hardest to convey the value of what we teach in order to give our students the best opportunity to see that there are things worth knowing, and that knowing them can enrich your life.

The rest is outside of our control and so we must not let it impact on the way we view our jobs or the way we teach. In the words of Marcus Aurelius:

"No matter what anyone says or does, my task is to be the emerald, my colour undiminished." *Meditations*, 7.15. Trans. Gregory Hays.

GETTING PRACTICAL PHILOSOPHY INTO THE CLASSROOM

Jules Evans

I would love there to be more practical philosophy in schools. At the moment, the teaching of ethics and philosophy in schools and universities is almost entirely theoretical. Students learn that philosophy is a matter of understanding and disputing concepts and theories, something that only involves the intellect, not your emotions, actions or life outside of the classroom.

This is a consequence of the splitting off of psychology from philosophy at the beginning of the 20th century. Philosophy lost touch with the central and immensely practical question of how to live well, and that ethical vacuum was filled by psychology, and even more by pharmacology.

Ironically, the most evidence-based talking therapy – Cognitive Behavioural Therapy – was directly inspired by ancient Greek philosophy, and uses many of its ideas and techniques. CBT picked up the baton which modern philosophy dropped, of trying to help ordinary people live happier lives. But it lacks the ethics, values and meaning dimension that ancient philosophy had.

Philosophy and psychology need each other. Philosophy without psychology is a brain in a vat, artificially cut off from emotions, actions and the habits of life. Psychology without ethics is a chicken without a head, focussed entirely on evidence without any clear sense of the goal. Practical philosophy is a bridge between the evidence-based techniques of psychology, and the Socratic questioning of philosophy.

I wish that, when I was suffering from social anxiety and depression at school, someone had told me about Stoic philosophy, and explained their idea that my emotions are connected to my beliefs and attitudes, and that we can transform our feelings by changing our beliefs. They might also have explained how CBT picked up the Stoics' ideas and tested them out. Instead, I had to find all this out for myself, and it took me several rather unhappy years. When I did finally come across ancient philosophy, it helped me enormously.

And I'm not alone in this. John Lloyd, the creator of Blackadder and QI, was a very bright boy at school, but never learned to reflect on the good life or how his thoughts create his subjective reality. He had to learn that himself, coming to philosophy after a five-year breakdown in his thirties. He now says: 'I think every child should learn Stoic philosophy.' *[See 'A Conversation with John Lloyd' in Part VIII]*. Making Stoicism part of the national curriculum is quite a big ask. But wouldn't it be great if there was at least *some* practical philosophy, some indication that philosophy can practically improve students' lives?

Eight Key Ideas To Get Across

If you're a teacher, and you want to do a class or philosophy club on Stoicism, here are **eight key ideas** that, speaking personally, I wish I'd come across at school:

1) It's not events that cause us suffering, but our opinion about events

People often think 'Stoic' means 'suppressing your emotions behind a stiff upper lip'. This is not what ancient Stoicism meant. The Stoics thought we could transform emotions by understanding how they're connected to our beliefs and attitudes. The quote above, from the philosopher Epictetus, is so powerful and useful – and it was the main inspiration for CBT. Often what causes us suffering is not a particular adverse event, but our opinion about it. We can make a difficult situation much worse by the attitude we bring to it. This doesn't mean relentlessly 'thinking positively' – it simply means being more mindful of how our attitudes and beliefs create our emotional reality. We don't realise that often we are the ones causing ourselves suffering through our thoughts. Have you noticed how people react very differently to exactly the same event, how some sink rapidly into despondency while others shrug it off? Perhaps we can learn to be more resilient and intelligent in how we react to events.

2) Our opinions are often unconscious, but we can bring them to consciousness by asking ourselves questions

Socrates said we sleepwalk through life, unaware of how we live and never asking ourselves if our opinions about life are correct or wise. CBT, likewise, suggests we have many cognitive biases – many of our deepest beliefs about ourselves and the world might be destructive and wrong. Yet we assume automatically they're true. The way to bring unconscious beliefs into consciousness is simply to ask yourself questions. Why am I feeling this strong emotional reaction? What interpretation or belief is leading to it? Is that belief definitely true? Where is the evidence for it? We can get into the practice of asking ourselves questions and examining our automatic interpretations. The Stoics used journals to keep track of their automatic responses and to examine them. CBT uses a similar technique. Maybe your students could keep a Stoic journal for a week.

3) We can't control everything that happens to us, but we can control how we react

This is another very simple and powerful idea from the Stoics, best presented by Epictetus, the slave-philosopher, who divided all human experience into two domains: things we can control and things we can't. We don't control other people, the weather, the economy, our bodies and health, our reputation, or things in the past and future. We can influence these things, but not entirely control them. The only thing we have complete control over is our beliefs – if we choose to exercise this control. But we often try to exert complete control over something external, and then feel insecure and angry when we fail. Or we fail to take responsibility for our own thoughts and beliefs, and use the outside world as an alibi. Focussing on what you control is a powerful way to reduce anxiety and assert autonomy in chaotic situations – you could use the stories of Viktor Frankl, the Holocaust survivor, or Sam Sullivan, the former Mayor of Vancouver, to illustrate this idea – they all faced profound adversity but managed to find a sense of autonomy in their response to it. *[See Stephen J. Costello's piece, 'A Sketch of Stoic Influences on Viktor Frankl's Logotherapy' in Part VI, and Jules Evans' piece, 'The Stoic Mayor' in Part IV].*

4) Choosing your perspective wisely

Every moment of the day, we can choose the perspective we take on life, like a film-director choosing the angle of a shot. What are you going to focus on? What's your angle on life?

A lot of the wisdom of Stoicism comes down to choosing your perspective wisely. One of the exercises the Stoics practiced was called the 'View From Above': if you're feeling stressed by some niggling annoyances, project your imagination into space and imagine the vastness of the universe. From that cosmic perspective, the annoyance doesn't seem that important anymore – you've made a molehill out of a mountain. Another technique the Stoics used (along with Buddhists and Epicureans) was bringing their attention back to the present moment, if they felt they were worrying too much about the future or ruminating over the past. Seneca told a friend: 'What's the point of dragging up sufferings that are over, of being miserable now because you were miserable then?'

5) The power of habits

One thing the Stoics got, which a lot of modern philosophy (and Religious Studies) misses with its focus on theory, is the importance of practice, training, repetition and, in a word, habits. It doesn't matter what theory you profess in the classroom if you don't embody it in your habits of thinking and acting. Because we're such forgetful creatures, we need to repeat ideas over and over until they become ingrained habits. It might be useful to talk about the Stoic technique of the maxim, how they'd encapsulate their ideas into brief memorisable phrases or proverbs (like 'Everything in moderation' or 'The best revenge is not to act the same way'), which they would repeat to themselves when needed. Stoics also carried around little handbooks with some of their favourite maxims in. What sayings do you find inspirational? Where could you put them up to remind yourself of them throughout the day?

6) Fieldwork

Another thing the Stoics got, which modern philosophy often misses, is the idea of fieldwork. One of my favourite quotes from Epictetus is: 'We might be fluent in the classroom but drag us out into practice and we're miserably shipwrecked'. Philosophy can't just be theory, it can't just be talk, it also has to be *askesis*, or practice. If you're trying to improve your temper, practice not losing it. If you're trying to rely less on comfort eating, practice eating less junk food. Seneca said: 'The Stoic sees all adversity as training'. I love the bit in *Fight Club* where students from Tyler Durden's school get sent out to do homework in the streets (even if the homework is a little, er, inappropriate, like intentionally losing a fight). Imagine if philosophy also gave us street homework, tailor-made for the habits we're trying to weaken or strengthen, like practicing asking a girl out, or practicing not gossiping about friends, or practicing being kind to someone every day. Imagine if people didn't think philosophy was 'just talking'. Diogenes the Cynic took *askesis* to the extreme of living in a barrel to prove how little we need to be happy – students tend to like stories about him.

7) Virtue is sufficient for happiness

All the previous main points are quite instrumental and value-neutral – that's why CBT has taken them up and turned them into a scientific therapy. But Stoicism wasn't just a feel-good therapy, it was an ethics, with a specific definition of the good life: the aim of life for Stoics was living in accordance with virtue. They believed that if you found the good life not in externals like wealth or power, but in doing *the right thing*, then you'd always be happy, because doing the right thing is always in your power and never subject to the whims of fortune. A demanding philosophy, and yet also in some ways true – doing the right thing is always in our power. So what are we worried about?

At this point your students might want to consider what they think is good or bad about this particular definition of the good life. Is it too focussed on the inner life? Are there external things we also think are necessary for the good life, such as friends or a free society? Can we live a good life even in those moments when we're not free, or we don't have many friends? What do your students think are the most important goods in life?

8) Our ethical obligations to our community

The Stoics pioneered the theory of cosmopolitanism – the idea that we have ethical obligations not just to our friends and family, but to our wider community, and even to the community of humanity. Sometimes our obligations might clash – between our friends and our country, or between our government and our conscience (for example, would we resist the Nazis if we grew up in 1930s Germany?) Do we really have moral obligations to people on the other side of the world? What about other species, or future generations? A useful exercise here, as Martha Nussbaum has suggested, is the Stoic exercise of the 'widening circles', imagining all the different wider communities that we're a part of.

PART SIX: STOICISM AND PSYCHOTHERAPY

DOES STOICISM WORK? STOICISM AND POSITIVE PSYCHOLOGY

Tim LeBon

Introduction: Stoicism isn't just a theory, it is also a set of practices aimed at helping people to lead better lives. A key question is whether Stoic practices work - does practising Stoicism actually help people? The scientific methods of psychology are the obvious place to turn to help answer this question. In this article, I will describe the work of the *Stoicism Today* team to use the methods of psychology to begin to answer the "Does Stoicism work?" question and suggest directions for future research. The last fifteen years have seen the growth of Positive Psychology, a branch of psychology aimed at providing a scientific understanding of what goes well in life and how to enhance it. I will argue that Positive Psychology can become more complete and wiser if it incorporates ideas from Stoicism.

Positive Psychology

Since its inception in 1998, Positive Psychology has spawned many experiments, articles, books and conferences. Whilst philosophers and self-help authors have long theorised about what we should do, Positive Psychology now proposes planned activities ("interventions") and tests them scientifically. One way is to ask people to carry out an intervention, measuring their well-being before and after to see its effect. Positive Psychology has already delivered substantial findings, including the following:

- Happiness and positive emotions such as joy, pride, love and awe don't just feel good, they also have positive consequences such as improved health and increased longevity, creativity and altruism.
- An important component of well-being is *flow*, which means being totally absorbed in what you are doing. Flow is distinct from pleasure because when you are absorbed in an activity you don't really *feel* anything.
- It is possible to cultivate a number of beneficial positive *attitudes*. These include hope, optimism, gratitude and a "growth mindset" (i.e. a belief that one's abilities are not fixed). These attitudes have been shown to lead to improved health, better work and academic performance, better self-esteem and greater resilience.
- A number of beneficial positive *behaviours* have been identified, including identifying and using your strengths and performing acts of kindness.
- A number of simple interventions have been shown to bring about increases in well-being in both the short term and at six-months follow up. Conversely some plausible interventions have been shown *not to* bring about lasting positive change.

There is now good evidence that studying Positive Psychology and applying its findings to oneself, to organisations and in education can lead to increased well-being. For a fuller review of Positive Psychology, the interested reader is referred to my new book, *Achieve Your Potential with Positive Psychology* (Hodder, 2014).

Philosophy and Positive Psychology

Whilst these developments are very much to be welcomed, there are some important *philosophical* questions to ask Positive Psychology, including:

- What precisely is well-being and what is the difference between well-being and related terms such as subjective well-being, flourishing, pleasure, enjoyment and happiness?
- Positive Psychology emphasises *feeling* good and *doing* good, but what is the place in Positive Psychology for virtue (i.e. *being* good)?
- Can positive attitudes and behaviours actually cause harm if they are carried out by someone who lacks virtue? For example, would you want a terrorist to use their strengths?
- Is, as many ancients thought, wisdom a particularly important virtue? Isn't it important not just to be hopeful and optimistic but to use these qualities wisely?
- Can practical ideas proposed by philosophers – such as the Stoics and Epicureans - be tested?
- Could empirically tested philosophical strategies help individuals be virtuous and wiser as well as feeling better and so strengthen Positive Psychology?

The remainder of this article will focus on the last two questions.

Stoicism Today and Putting Stoicism to the Test

Stoicism is a good candidate for inclusion in Positive Psychology both because of its broadly therapeutic intent and the plethora of specific, testable strategies to be found in the writings of Marcus Aurelius, Seneca and, particularly, Epictetus. Under the leadership of Professor Christopher Gill based at the University of Exeter, the *Stoicism Today* team, including the current author, has made a start at putting Stoicism to the test. In this section, I will briefly summarise our findings. For a more detailed account, see LeBon (2014a)

In the latest 2013 study, participants, recruited from the general public as well as Stoic interest groups, were provided with a free downloadable booklet featuring Stoic readings and exercises, many of which were available as audio recordings. In addition a blog was maintained and participants were encouraged to communicate with each other using social media. Central to the empirical study was the suggested programme of meditations and exercises for "Stoic week". Each day had a specific Stoic theme, and an early morning and late evening meditation connected the daily theme with more general Stoic ideas.

Amongst the suggested exercises were:

- An early morning meditation, focussing on a Stoic principle such as "focussing only on things under our control", or "rehearsing dealing with possible challenges in the day ahead in a Stoic way".
- A late evening meditation, reviewing the day in terms of how well one has dealt with challenges in a Stoic way, learning what one has done well but also cultivating the intention to do better the next day.
- Daily exercises on the following themes: What is in our power?; Stoic self-discipline and simplicity; the Stoic reserve clause; Stoic mindfulness; Emotions and adversity; philanthropy and the View from Above.
- A Stoic monitoring sheet, helping to cultivate an awareness of what is and what is not in our power.

Participants were asked to take various questionnaires assessing well-being and their levels of Stoicism both before and after taking part in Stoic week.

Stoicism Today's Testing of Stoicism: The Results

Our findings supported the view that Stoicism is helpful – Stoicism passed its initial test. Participants reported a 14% improvement in life satisfaction, a 9% increase in positive emotions and an 11% decrease in negative emotions.

These findings suggest a significant positive effect of practising Stoicism, and also go some way to dispelling some of the more frequent criticisms of Stoicism, such as that it is a joyless philosophy (joy increased the most of all emotions) or that it is too pessimistic (optimism increased by 18%). In addition the study confirmed some positive expectations of Stoicism. Stoicism does indeed seem to increase contentment and reduce anger. The findings also supported the view that Stoicism not only increases well-being but also enhances virtue - 56% of participants gave themselves a mark of 80% or more when asked whether it had made them a better person and made them wiser.

As well as measuring changes in well-being, the *Stoicism Today* project has also attempted to measure the relationship between well-being and Stoic attitudes and behaviours. In order to do this, a scale, The Stoic Attitudes and Behaviours Scales (SABS) has been developed and piloted. By giving participants the SABS questionnaire along with other well-being scales, it is possible to determine the relationship between elements of Stoicism and well-being, and thereby, potentially to identify Stoicism's "active ingredients". Most Stoic *behaviours* have proved to be positively associated with well-being. Many Stoic *attitudes* are also positively associated with well-being, but less so than behaviours. Some non-Stoic behaviours attitudes, such as doing what is enjoyable and comfortable rather than the right thing, proved to be negatively associated with well-being.

The elements of Stoicism that proved the most beneficial were:

- Stoic mindfulness - making an effort to pay continual attention to the nature of my judgments and actions.
- Stoic disputation of thoughts - reminding oneself that an upsetting thought is just an impression in my mind and not the thing it claims to represent.

- Affinity with others - thinking of oneself as part of the human race, in the same way that a limb is a part of the human body.
- Stoic Premeditation - trying to anticipate future misfortunes and rehearse rising above them.

Future Directions

Whilst these findings are certainly encouraging, more research is required for it to reach the most rigorous scientific standards. Priorities include:

- Performing more rigorous, controlled experiments. The findings would be strengthened if follow-ups were performed (e.g. at 3 or 6 months) and if control groups were established.
- Further Development of the Stoic attitudes and behaviours scale (SABS). The SABS scale is a promising instrument both to measure adherence to Stoicism and its association with well-being. The scale would benefit from refinement, including simplification of the language used and a further round of feedback from those who identify themselves as Stoic.
- Longitudinal testing of SABS findings. The SABS findings are correlational i.e., they show a relationship between well-being and Stoicism. They do not prove that being more Stoic brings about the changes in well-being. One way to address this would be to compare changes in well-being between participants instructed to develop very specific Stoic attitudes and behaviours. For instance it could compare instructing one set of participants to engage in Stoic mindfulness with another instructed to do just a Stoic premeditation.
- Further refinement of materials and programmes. There is a close analogy between the idea of developing Stoic-inspired programmes from Stoicism with developing mindfulness programmes from Buddhism. Mindfulness-based programmes have been shown to reduce the recur-

rence of depression and are now very popular - they are even available in the NHS. Researchers have based these programmes on a subset of Buddhist practices, and geared them to specific groups. In the same way programmes could be refined for particular problems most likely to benefit from Stoicism, e.g. anger management and those suffering long-term conditions such as diabetes and coronary heart disease.

Stoicism as a part of Positive Psychology

Whilst further research is desirable, I believe enough evidence has been collected to justify including Stoic exercises in the arsenal of evidence-based techniques to enhance well-being. In this final section I will make some brief remarks to suggest that Stoicism may have particular value in helping Positive Psychology address helping people to be virtuous and wise *as well as* feeling good and doing good.

Positive Psychologists engaged in a literature search on virtues and came up with six virtues including the four cardinal virtues of ancient Greece (wisdom, courage, self-control and justice). However, whilst Stoics and other Greek and Roman thinkers mostly thought that all of these virtues were required to lead the good life, positive psychologists instead encourage people to identify their strengths and use their top strengths more. Strengths are more specific, operationalised versions of virtues – for instance the virtue of wisdom has been broken down into strengths of creativity, curiosity, judgement, love of learning and perspective. There is good evidence that using one's strengths in new ways increases one's own sense of well-being. It is not clear though whether it is the best way of making one more virtuous. There is a strong argument to suggest that virtue may require the opposite – focussing more on the moral qualities one lacks. For example, if a man is courageous but lacks self-control, should he perform more acts of courage or try to develop his self-control? More questionable still is whether they can perform true acts of courage or self-control without possessing wisdom.

As Socrates argued in the *Laches,* retreating can show more courage than attacking, depending on the circumstances. Wisdom is required to decide which acts are virtuous.

Being a virtue-based philosophy, Stoicism is well-placed to fill in this gap in Positive Psychology. Stoics require individuals to develop virtues, even if they are not their strengths and provides exercises to enable them to do so. In encouraging people to control only what they can control and consider the welfare of others, Stoicism can also help people develop wisdom. Stoicism offers Positive Psychology and the individual the opportunity to develop their character as well as increase their well-being.

References:

LeBon, T., Report on Exeter University "Stoic week" 2013: http://blogs.exeter.ac.uk/stoicismtoday/files/2014/02/Stoic-Week-Report-2013-Final.pdf. 2014a.

LeBon, T., *Achieve Your Potential with Positive Psychology.* Hodder: 2014b.

The Stoicism Today Team. *Stoic Week Booklet:* http://blogs.exeter.ac.uk/stoicismtoday/files/2013/11/Stoic_Week_2013_Handbook.pdf. 2013.

NB. The Stoic Attitudes and Behaviours Scale, and other questionnaires mentioned, can be found in Tim LeBon's *Report on Exeter University "Stoic Week" 2013.*

A SKETCH OF THE STOIC INFLUENCES ON VIKTOR FRANKL'S LOGOTHERAPY

Stephen J. Costello.

For centuries, Stoicism was the most influential philosophy in the Graeco-Roman world. Founded by Zeno of Citium in the fourth century BC who taught from a stoa (a painted porch or colonnade) in Athens, it was to attract into its ranks men as diverse as Epictetus the former slave, Seneca the statesman and Marcus Aurelius the emperor. In the context of the Ancient classical Greek tradition, philosophy was understood to be a therapy of the soul and the site of spiritual exercises, persuasively argued for and highlighted by Pierre Hadot in his *What is Ancient Philosophy?* and *Philosophy as a Way of Life*.

It was Stoicism, arguably, that was the preeminent practical philosophy of the time. This older view of philosophy as *praxis*, as a care of the self or cure of the soul, may be traced back to Socrates' maieutic method (meaning to give birth, in this case, to ideas) and more systematically to Plato's understanding of the nature of philosophy itself (*'therapie der Seele'* or 'therapy of the Soul'). This applied interpretation was alive and well with the Stoics but ruptured in the Middle Ages before returning in the nineteenth-century with Nietzsche and Kierkegaard and in the twentieth-century with various thinkers such as Viktor E. Frankl, Eric Voegelin, Jan Patocka, Michel Foucault, Ludwig Wittgenstein, and others who retrieved the 'ancient consolation'. That said, there were some notable exceptions down the centuries such as Michel de Montaigne and the Earl of Shaftesbury.

In this present paper, I want to state the case for some Stoic sources underlying Frankl's logotherapy and existential analysis.

This takes the form of a preliminary sketch or outline rather than analysis or exhaustive exegesis. There have been hints in the literature on the subject, threads to follow, sparse as they are, interestingly and curiously however, not from Frankl himself. For example, William S. Sahakian in 'Logotherapy's Place in Philosophy', has written: 'Logotherapy and stoicism share a number of ideas' (work cited, p. 54) and points to two such ones: the existence of attitudinal values and the non-existence of purposeless evil. For the Stoics, as for Frankl, all suffering can be made meaningful. Sahakian states: 'Frankl's attitudinal value theory is unquestionably stoic in character' (*ibid.*, p. 55). Both logotherapy and Stoicism would argue that if a situation cannot be changed, we are challenged to change ourselves; a person has the freedom to alter his attitude to his problem. This is essential to both schools.

Epictetus exclaimed that the essence of good and evil lies in the (attitude of) the will in *Discourses* 2.1. Similarly, Frankl advances the notion that where we can no longer control our fate and reshape it, we must be able to accept it (see, for example, *Psychotherapy and Existentialism*). To an extent, the sting of life lies in a state of mind, in a condition of the soul. Conditions and circumstances do not determine me; I decide them.

The role of the 'will' has a prominent and paramount place in both Stoic philosophy and logotherapy. Indeed, two of the three pillars on which logotherapy is constructed concern the will, viz., freedom of the will and the will to meaning. Both schools stress that the will is unconquerable – invincible and inviolate – and that a person needs to transform his circumstances or, if he can't, alter his attitude towards them. The will ultimately rests within our power – what Frankl called 'the last of the human freedoms'. To take an example, Socrates was resolute in the face of his own execution despite

Anytus and Meletus trying to break his spirit. As Socrates realised: 'Anytus and Meletus have the power to put me to death, but hurt me they cannot'. In logotherapy, the exercise of the will not only effects a change of attitude but is also capable of producing self-detachment/distancing, through the technique of paradoxical intention (indeed, there are many comparisons between logotherapy and CBT, although there are some important differences too - the main ones being that logotherapy and existential analysis take unconscious mental processes seriously as well as the spiritual sphere). What is common to Stoicism and logotherapy are multiple exercises such as the review and preview of the day (in logotherapy) and the evening reflection (in Stoicism): a kind of examen of consciousness.

Both Marcus Aurelius and Frankl are pioneers of philosophical practice. There is a strong connection between the spiritual exercises of the ancient philosophers, particularly the Stoics and the methods and techniques of Franklian logotherapy and existential analysis (LTEA). We may list some of them:

- Socratic dialogue (drawing out what is latent through open-ended questions)
- Modification of attitudes (aim of therapy here is attitudinal change)
- Paradoxical Intention (wishing to have happen the thing you fear most: has a 75% clinical success rate)
- Dereflection (a reorientation of the mind onto something more meaningful)
- Existential Analysis of Dreams (dreams have always been the 'royal road' to the unconscious)

These logotherapeutical methods have always been part and parcel of ancient philosophy even if they have received different names. Logotherapy is a type of spiritual and Socratic midwifery. As Reinard Zaiser writes: 'You can find dereflexion, for example, in the meditations by the Roman emperor and stoic philosopher Marcus Aurelius' (work cited, p. 84). Both systems emphasise the role of attitudinal modulation, and paradoxical intention, arguably the most famous of logotherapeutical techniques, has its precursor and parallel in the ancient paradoxical suggestion therapy. There is a case to be made for Socrates being the first logotherapist!

My aim below is simply to show ten points of commonality and connection, especially in the context of some other commentators correctly drawing a link between Stoic philosophy and cognitive-behavioural therapy. It points the way to further elucidation.

A Comparison between Stoicism and Logotherapy's Fundamentals

Stoics: Stoics see the world as a single community, in which all men are brothers (*cosmopolis*).

Logotherapy: Frankl speaks of 'monoanthropism' ('universal humanity').

Stoics: The universe is ruled by a supreme providence – the *Logos*/ divine reason/ nature/spirit.

Logotherapy: *Logos* is meaning. We should pay heed to the voice of our conscience as it is the organ of meaning – it comes to us as a 'hint from Heaven'.

Stoics: Our duty is to live in accordance with the divine will; to live in line with nature's laws, its inborn gift of reason (the divine element).

Logotherapy: Flourishing is living in accordance with all three dimensions: *soma* (body), *psyche* (mind) and *noös* (rational spirit).

Stoics: We need to discipline the passions, realising that reason is higher than instincts, inclinations, and impulsions (vigilance).

Logotherapy: The passions need to be integrated, and the unconscious made conscious. *Noös* (the noetic core of resilience) transcends *soma*.

Stoics: We must resign ourselves or accept what fate (*Fortuna*) may bring us.

Logotherapy: We need to harness the 'will to meaning' and the 'defiant power of the human spirit' to deal with 'blows of fate', without flinching.

Stoics: We must not set too high a value on things that can be taken from us (externals), but cultivate a cosmic consciousness and focus on inner values.

Logotherapy: Man must orient himself to the eternal such as the True, the Good and the Beautiful more than the ephemeral and put things in proper perspective (dereflection).

Stoics: We are disturbed not by the things themselves but by the view we take towards them (our interpretations).

Logotherapy: What is important is how we respond rather than react to things (the attitude we adopt or stance we assume).

Stoics: The aim is to procure peace of mind and freedom from fear. Moral goodness (virtue) is the end. Happiness is a by-product.

Logotherapy: Happiness is a by-product of meaningful existence. To find it we must forget about it.

Stoics: The *summum bonum* (supreme good) is a combination of the four cardinal virtues: wisdom or *sophia* (moral and spiritual insight), courage (fortitude), justice (fair dealing), and temperance (self-control).

Logotherapy: The essence of human existence is ethical and spiritual self-transcendence, as we journey from the existential vacuum to ethical values.

Stoics: Philosophy is both practical and therapeutic – the site of spiritual exercises, whose aim is to form more than inform.

Logotherapy: Logotherapy is a form of Socratic or noetic therapy and a philosophy of life, the ultimate aim of which is self-transformation.

References

Allport, G.W., 'Preface', *Man's Search for Meaning*. Rider, 2004 (1959).

Aurelius, M., *Meditations*. Everyman's Library, 1946.

Epictetus, *Discourses*. Books 1-4. Dover Publications, 2004.

Epictetus, *The Handbook* (*The Echeiridion*). Hackett Publishing, 1983.

Frankl, V., *Man's Search for Meaning*. Rider, 2004 (1959).

Frankl, V., *Psychotherapy and Existentialism*. Washington Square Press, 1967.

Hadot, P., *Philosophy as a Way of Life*. Blackwell Publishing, 1995.

Hadot, P., *What is Ancient Philosophy?* Harvard University Press, 2002.

Hadot, P., *The Inner Citadel: The Meditations of Marcus Aurelius*. Harvard University Press, 2001.

Sahakian, W.S., 'Logotherapy's Place in Philosophy', *Logotherapy in Action*. Ed. Fabry J., Bulka R. Sahakian W.S., Foreword by Viktor Frankl. Jason Aronson, 1979.

Zaiser, R., 'Working on the Noetic Dimension of Man: Philosophical Practice, Logotherapy, and Existential Analysis', *Philosophical Practice*, July, 2005: 1(2).

MY RETURN TO MENTAL HEALTH WITH CBT AND STOICISM

James Davinport

A year ago my whole world collapsed. In hindsight, I can say that I should have seen it coming - the breakdown had been building up for years: month by month vestiges of my self were chipped away, until finally, it felt like there was not really a 'me' there that I could recognize anymore. At work, in the lower echelons of a high-powered business, I had driven myself down into the dust. I had worked seven days a week for years, often into the early hours of the morning. By the end, nothing on the computer screen in front of me made any sense and nothing I read made any sense. I dreaded the regular presentations I had to make at work: I felt like each and every one I gave was a 'failure' (even though the peer-assessment I received indicated the exact opposite). I didn't want to see people, and I lashed out at family and friends. One evening, I found myself kicking a chair in my living room for no reason. Luckily, my lodger was not in the room at the time! During the day, I would slip away from the office to cry in a nearby park. My head raced with negative thought after negative thought, many of which were so irrational, that it was upsetting just to have them. Often, in my mind's eye, I'd see visions of myself crying out for help.

But it was the physical symptoms that made me finally shout 'stop': the dizziness, exhaustion, tender muscles that would suddenly seize up, the panic attacks, the inability to remember or concentrate, the heart palpitations, and digestive difficulties for months on end. Whereas the mental symptoms could not, sadly, curtail my self-destructive ways, my body, the health of which suddenly seemed so absolutely *vital*, was what finally forced me to reassess what I was doing.

So I did what seemed the unthinkable: I quit my job, gathered my savings, and set about recovering.

This article is about how I have made that recovery, and will, I hope, be of use to others who find themselves in similar situations to the one I found myself in.

* * *

At first, I had little idea what was wrong with me: I just felt that 'everything' was wrong with me. I wondered if I had 'CFS', the dreaded 'Chronic Fatigue Syndrome', and whether I would be condemned to years, decades possibly, of extreme tiredness. Being in my late forties, I worried if anything, realistically, could be done at this stage: I'd spent years doing the wrong thing, and now, how could I possibly expect any real change for the better? But, deep down inside me, there grew the greatest determination I have ever experienced to *get better*.

I had tried meditation for the first time a few months before my break-down but I was so anxious that, after each session of mindfulness meditation I was closer to a panic attack than before it. (Later, I learned that this was brought on by a rather curious form of OCD, or Obsessive Compulsive Disorder, I had developed, called 'sensorimotor OCD', which leads to high levels of anxiety as a result of paying attention to bodily sensations). The present moment hardly seems a joyful place when your head is racing with negative thoughts and turbulent emotions. It became clear to me that 'accepting' these thoughts and feelings non-judgmentally was not what I needed to do: I needed to *change* them.

Recovering with CBT

I'd long heard about CBT, or Cognitive Behavioural Therapy, but had never really considered it for myself. But early on in my determination to recover, when I was idly browsing the shelves in a London bookstore, I came across a *Teach Yourself CBT* book. I thought 'Why not?', and bought it. This was the best purchase of my life. I was determined to commit wholeheartedly to what the book taught me, building on each lesson bit by bit.

CBT requires continuous training. Over the last months, I have learned many helpful techniques, but here I'll just outline some of the most fundamental practices.

The first exercise was to 'reframe' the thoughts I had, and see them as something outside of myself which was 'up for debate'. Thus, I would rewrite

'I feel anxious that my future holds nothing good',

as

'Anxiety tells me my future holds nothing good'.

The process of doing this in itself gave me a huge sense of achievement: instead of letting Negative Automatic Thoughts (or NATs) ruin the day, I was capturing them at their inception and *stopping them in their tracks*. The process of writing the NATs down was important too - it is good to get such thoughts 'outside of yourself' and onto a piece of paper.

The second exercise focussed on applying what CBT calls 'General Thinking Errors' to each negative thought: was I thinking 'in extremes' with no shades of complexity or nuance? Was I 'overgeneralising' to assume that one bad incident should apply to everything else, *forever*? Was I 'filtering out the positive', only looking at the negative aspects of the situation? Was

I 'jumping to conclusions', 'mind reading' or 'fortune telling'? For another week, I methodically challenged each negative thought in light of these thinking errors, growing more and more in confidence each day.

The third exercise, which combines all of these together, was about replacing negative thoughts with more realistic, balanced ones, noticing the effect of doing this on my mood and feelings. Let me give a (made-up) example:

Thoughts: "I made a complete fool of myself at the party. Everyone thought I was an idiot." How much do I believe this? 74/100.

Feelings: Isolation, upset, like no one will like me.

Alternative thoughts: "Objectively speaking, there was only one real awkward moment in the party, and I'm probably blowing even that out of proportion. Other people had awkward moments at the party too, and they just laughed them off - I guess a bit of awkwardness is a part of life! The rest of it went quite well, and I actually got on particularly well with two new people. All in all, there were more positives than negatives to the evening. How much do I believe this? 95/100

Feelings: Contented, a more balanced perspective, like one awkward moment doesn't put people off liking me. How much do I believe the old thought now? 0/100

I have practised this particular technique ever since. I have come to love the challenge of doing it. It feels rather like 'gardening', as if challenging negative thoughts is like clearing out weeds. What I also like about this method is that is not about replacing negative thoughts with 'positive thinking' for its own sake, but rather with balanced, more accurate thinking, which accepts nuanced understandings of situations. And the great thing is that, today, my thinking in general is more balanced in the first place, and reflects more accurately *how the world works*.

The Power of Underlying Beliefs

For CBT, the mind is like an onion: the thoughts we have are at the very outermost 'layer' and, that we have them at all, usually depends on some 'underlying belief'. For example, if you feel panicky when in social situations, as I do, you might have the underlying belief that 'I'm unlikeable' or 'Other people usually are judgemental and unfriendly'. And those kinds of beliefs feed into your behaviours: you find yourself *avoiding* others so as not to *confirm* your underlying beliefs. It's a self-perpetuating cycle of negativity that needs to be broken.

As I uncovered my underlying beliefs, I began to detect certain overarching patterns in my thinking. After some research, it became clear that I had Social Anxiety Disorder (a deep seated fear of rejection and humiliation) and serious problems with Perfectionism (where one's self-worth is dependent on achieving rigid, wholly unrealistic goals in one or two areas of one's life). In addition, albeit in a more minor way, it also become clear that hypochondria, agoraphobia, PTSD and various kinds of OCD were also in the mix. Sometimes you have to have a sense of humour when faced with all your neuroses! But luckily, especially for someone new to CBT like myself, there were CBT books available for each of these problems. And let me tell you that that is a *relief.* When you need help with these kinds of issues, you need books that deal with the problems head-on, backed up by *evidence*. I took a long-term view and set about changing each of these areas systematically.

This process is still ongoing. Challenging these underlying beliefs takes time, but it is a process that one comes to value and take pride in. It involves a *lot* of behavioural experiments, in which you directly confront your fears and constantly re-evaluate the beliefs that fuel them. It also involves learning a lot about human psychology, and how behaviours feed into emotions and thoughts and vice versa. It's a highly rewarding journey. But today, I can safely say that over the last few months the balance has tipped:

- From being generally 'on-edge' and feeling scared when out and about, I have gone to *love* being out and about.
- Whereas before, I would have quickly withdrawn into my shell in social situations and felt 'isolated', I've now become increasingly confident in meeting new people, and tend to focus on the positives of each event afterwards and not on a negative 'post mortem'.
- Now that I'm in work again, I don't drive myself non-stop. Now, my self-worth is derived from the whole spectrum of my life, not just my work-related achievements. I can knock off without the slightest shred of guilt at not checking my email until 9 AM the next morning.
- From being fearful that I had several kinds of serious illness, such thoughts now rarely cross my mind. In fact, these days I laugh on the few occasions I have those thoughts.
- The panic attacks have simply *disappeared*.

A year ago all this seemed impossible even to dream of. Now, it seems hard to countenance the kind of fears I had a year ago: was that *really* me? Back then, it seemed like the world was a harsh and horrible place. But, in fact, the outside world has not *changed* - rather, my *relationship* to it has changed. And that I achieved myself.

Recovering with Stoicism

Early on in my journey with CBT, I encountered Epictetus's key idea, from *Handbook* §5, that 'We are not disturbed by events but by our opinions about events'. As is well known, and as I found out, this was a key idea behind CBT. This fact made me curious about Stoicism, and, after some research, I read some books and used some online materials (including those on the *Stoicism Today* blog). As a philosophy, it really resonated with me.

But, I'll be frank upfront. Had I picked up a book on Stoicism a year ago, rather than CBT, I don't think I would have made the great strides of progress that I have made. I'd probably have made some progress, but only a fraction of what I have made. Why? Because Stoicism was not developed specifically to tackle Social Anxiety Disorder, Agoraphobia, Perfectionism or Hypochondria! The idea that Stoicism is a 'Therapy for the Soul', and the key saying within Stoicism by Epictetus which I just quoted above, of course, make it *seem* similar to CBT. But that doesn't make it psychotherapy, in the modern sense, which is concerned with treating specific problems. In contrast, Stoicism is 'psychotherapeutic' in the sense that is concerned with developing 'good flow of life', based on coherent ethical values, rather than a more turbulent 'all over the place' kind of life with suspect or ill-thought-out values. It is also psychotherapeutic in the idea that certain value-judgements (such as 'I need money to be happy') can lead to psychological disturbances that can be removed with shifting to value virtue instead. In other words, Stoicism is essentially different as it is about ethics. And, the key thing is that having Social Anxiety Disorder or Hypochondria are not *ethical* failings. When someone wants help with recovering from panic attacks, help them to recover from panic attacks but don't ask them to define 'virtue'!

So how, you might ask, did Stoicism help me to recover? CBT is immensely helpful up to a point. It does its job wonderfully but it is necessarily defined in relation to removing something *negative*. Whilst this process in itself can lead to more positive things - self-confidence, and the enjoyment of parts of your life that once made you feel fearful, CBT does not give any advice on how to live your life in an overarching way, or on what you should value in life in general.

As I cleared out all the 'negative weeds' bit by bit, I found that there was a certain hole, or absence, within me. And the question that was emerging was: what is the mast, or rock, by which I can live my life? And that's where Stoicism came in: it filled up the space that had been created by rooting out the negative weeds.

Although my journey with Stoicism is in its early days, there are three key things that I have taken away which have started forming the bedrock of my life:

- *The focus on 'what is up to me':* for me, this is about understanding that the most important thing in life is valuing keeping your integrity in how you go about things. You don't need external events to be like this or like that - purpose comes instead from valuing retaining your integrity in response to those events.

- *The Examined Life:* Every evening, I practise the evening philosophical review. I praise myself for what I did well, and highlight areas that need to improve. No longer is my day just one seamless 'blur'. Now I have sense of my 'overall life narrative', of what I'm seeking to do, of certain ethical precepts, as simple as the importance of valuing friends and family, which can guide me each day. In the evening, I become, as the *Stoic Week 2013 Handbook* puts it, akin to a 'Philosophical Counselor' to myself.

- *Happiness through cultivating philanthropy:* The Stoic idea that we should seek to cultivate affection towards others has been a powerful influence on my life. Hierocles' circles have been especially helpful in doing this. It has led me to prioritize cultivating relationships, friendships and community, and to the realization that in those areas, it would seem, is indeed where happiness can be found.

There is more to delve into with Stoicism - I still couldn't define 'virtue' if you gave me a million dollars! - and possibly other philosophies, but, for the moment, the values by which I will live my life are slowly, but surely, coming together. Whilst CBT gave me my life back, by removing the negative things that had been obstructing it, Stoicism is providing reflection for the meaning or basis of my life *as a whole*.

* * *

Of course, there still are some bad moments. I am only one year into my recovery. But I recognize those moments much more quickly now, and know what to do. When I look back at the kind of thoughts that used to plague me not so long ago, I have visible proof of how far I have come in so short a time. Physically, I am much better too. So many of the symptoms I had experienced before have simply disappeared, thanks, I believe, to having a much calmer mind and to having the time to commit to a sensible exercise regimen. And, in case you are wondering, I now practice mindfulness meditation again, and it does not leave me anxious! It has once more become an important part of my life.

I hope that, in writing this piece, if there is someone out there who finds himself or herself in a similar position to the one I was in a year ago, that they can know that it is possible to change. The simple fact that it is in one's power only to tend well to certain parts of your life - thoughts, intentions and actions - might seem limiting.

But I know now, firmly from my own experience, that focussing on those things is the *most powerful thing you can do*.

PART SEVEN: STOICISM AND MINDFULNESS

MINDFUL VIRTUE: EASTERN MEDITATION FOR STOIC ETHICS

Ben Butina

Seriously, guys.

With the flood of books and articles coming out every day on gracklene, it's really about time that we hash this thing out from a Stoic perspective. Can gracklene really help a person become more virtuous? If so, how? And how does gracklene fit with ancient Stoic practices? Are we just pulling out the parts of gracklene that we like and throwing out the rest because we find them inconvenient?

At this point, you're probably asking, "What the hell *is* gracklene*, anyway?" Good question. Before we get into that, though, re-read the previous paragraph, replacing the word *gracklene* with the word *mindfulness.*

Gracklene is a completely unfamiliar word, so it sends up a red flag. You probably wouldn't try to have a conversation about gracklene without first clarifying its definition. *Mindfulness*, on the other hand, is becoming a very familiar word, and we tend to have conversations about it as if we shared a common understanding of what it means. That's where we run into trouble.

According to the *Oxford English Dictionary*, the English word "mindfulness" has been around at least since 1530 A.D. and was used several times in the King James Bible (1611 A.D.). Consider, for example:

'He is the Lord our God; his judgments are in all the earth. Be ye *mindful* always of his covenant; the word which he commanded to a thousand generations; Even of the covenant which he made with Abraham, and of his oath unto Isaac.' 1 *Chronicles* 16:14-16.

Needless to say, it didn't have any Buddhist connotations at the time, but simply referred to being aware of something, remembering it and paying attention to it. The Buddhist connotations of the word didn't kick in, in the West, until 1910, when Rhys Davids, a scholar of early Buddhism, appropriated *mindfulness* to stand in for the Pali word *sati* in his hugely influential English translation of the *Satipatthana Sutta* (*The Discourse on the Four Foundations of Mindfulness*). Although *sati* originally meant 'memory', its use in early Buddhist writings is subtle, complex, and varied. Bhante Sujato, for example, argues that 'Sati' means 'sustained attention', as part of a process that is aimed at leading the mind to purification, and insight into the Buddha's Noble Eight-fold Path.

But the definition of mindfulness that we use most frequently now in Western countries bears little resemblance to the earlier English-language definition of mindfulness and is not a direct translation of any single Pali word. It is usually, instead, some variation or other of the definition offered by pioneering secular mindfulness teacher Jon Kabat-Zinn:

'Mindfulness means paying attention in a particular way; on purpose, in the present moment, and nonjudgmentally.'

Sounds familiar, right? But you'll find that the Kabat-Zinn definition gets mutilated quite a bit in the press. Here is how mindfulness was described in the five most recent popular articles about mindfulness I could find on Google News:

'The most basic definition of mindfulness? It's simply paying attention.' Melanie Harth, Ph.D., LMHC, *Huffington Post*.

'Simply put, mindfulness is the act of focussing on the present moment in a non-judgmental way.' Janet Singer, *PsychCentral*.

'I practise mindfulness, which involves letting my garbage go through my brain but always bringing my focus to my breathing.' Ruby Wax, *The Telegraph*.

'…a practiced nonjudgmental in-the-moment awareness rooted in meditation, Buddhism and yoga…' Todd Essig, *Forbes Magazine*.

'Mindfulness is a way to "detach from the literal junk that comes through your mind" by observing thoughts in a non-judgmental, non-emotional way…' Eden Kozlowski, *Akron Beacon Journal*.

Are these five people all talking about the same thing? Maybe. But they sure aren't speaking the same language. Two of the definitions above suggest that our thoughts are bad ("garbage," "literal junk"), which is problematic. One of them ("simply paying attention") simplifies the concept to the point of meaninglessness. None of them, including the respected Kabat-Zinn version, gives us much of a clue as to what we're supposed to be paying attention *to*.

If we're going to talk about how mindfulness can be used in a Stoic context, clearly, we need to settle on a shared understanding of what the word means. The definitions discussed above are simple and accessible, but ultimately vague and unsatisfying. I propose that we adopt the definition of *mindful awareness* offered by American meditation teacher Shinzen Young, namely, that it is:

'...three attentional skills working together: Concentration Power, Sensory Clarity, and Equanimity.'

Right off the bat, you can tell that it's not as simple as the definitions we looked at above. It's going to require a little unpacking, but stay with me: it will pay off.

Young elaborates:

'You can think of Concentration Power as the ability to focus on what you consider to be relevant at a given time. You can think of Sensory Clarity as the ability to keep track of what you're actually experiencing in the moment. You can think of Equanimity as the ability to allow sensory experience to come and go without push and pull.'

Concentration, therefore, is simply being able to pay attention to what you deem relevant. *Sensory Clarity* is the ability to keep track of all the components of your experience with high magnification and high resolution - it allows you to track all the external and internal "bits" that make up your sensory experience of the world. *Equanimity* allows you to experience those "bits" without trying to push them away, grasp onto them, or spin them into a story. In addition, Young doesn't define concentration, clarity, and equanimity as states or traits, but as *skills*. And like all skills, you can improve them with practice. But why would a Stoic *want* to? Because *mindful awareness increases our ability to live virtuously.*

Mindful awareness is not, therefore, itself a virtue, but it is a powerful *enabler* of virtue. It improves our ability to act according to our intentions by clearing away the obstacles that prevent us from acting rationally. Here are three scenarios to give you an idea of how this might work:

- You're sitting at the dinner table with your family, but you're only vaguely aware that anyone is talking to you. Your mind is awash in memories of your day at work, worries about the next day, and fantasies about your upcoming vacation. You want to pay attention to the people you love, but you lack *concentration*.

- You hear a crash coming from the next room. Your immediate reaction is to fly off in a rage. You storm into the room screaming, "What the hell is going on in here?!?" You know you should act calmly to make sure no one was hurt, but you are overwhelmed by emotion (i.e., "passion") because you lack the *sensory clarity* necessary to break your reaction down into its component parts where they are easier to deal with. Instead, everything just sort of comes at you in a big, tangled ball of overwhelm.

- You ask a question of someone at work and they answer in a hurried fashion. You immediately begin telling yourself a story about their reaction. Soon you've invented an entire drama in which you've assumed that they're angry with you about something you've done...but what? You lack the *equanimity* necessary to experience the situation simply for what it is without inventing a mental story to go with it.

In all three cases, your intentions were good. You wanted to act with virtue, but you got overwhelmed and reacted instead of responding reasonably. Now let's look at the same three situations with a higher level of mindful awareness:

- You're sitting at the dinner table with your family and your mind is awash with memories, planning, and fantasy. You hear someone say your name and you're able to leave your thoughts aside and focus your attention entirely on the person speaking to you.

- You hear a crash coming from the next room. You become aware of mental images (a shattered television screen), mental talk ("What they hell are they doing in there?!") and physical body sensations (a tightening of the stomach muscles, a racing heartbeat), and you're able to deal with them without being overwhelmed. You move swiftly but calmly into the next room to make sure no one is hurt.

- You ask a question of someone at work and get a brusque response. You become aware of your reactions (mental image, mental talk, physical body sensation) and allow them to come and go without attaching to them and spinning them into a troubling story.

Here again, your intentions are good, but now you have the skills necessary to act virtuously without getting swept away by passion or distraction. The software (Stoicism) is the same, but the upgraded hardware (mindful awareness) has allowed you to act according to your intentions.

In short, mindful awareness gives you the ability to *respond* rather than simply *react*. And that's a key skill to have, when you are trying to lead a Stoic life.

Gracklene is just a word I made up by combining the brand names of things I found in my kitchen.

References

Davids, R., *Translation of the* Satipatthana Sutta (*Discoures on the Four Establishments of Mindfulness*):
http://buddhistlibraryonline.com/index.php/dighanikaya/mahavaggapali/dn22-mahasatipatthana-sutta/58-mahasatipatthana1.
De Rosée, S., *Ruby Wax on Depression, Mindfulness and Prada Handbags*: http://www.telegraph.co.uk/culture/books/authorinterviews/11015928/Ruby-Wax-on-depression-mindfulness-and-Prada-handbags.html..
Essig, T., *Google's Gopi Kallayil On the Business Value of Mindfulness*: http://www.forbes.com/sites/toddessig/2014/07/26/googles-gopi-kallayil-on-the-business-value-of-mindfulness/.

Harth, M., *Mindfulness for Success: Top 3 Management Tips*: http://www.huffingtonpost.com/melanie-harth-phd-lmhc/mindfulness-for-success-t_b_5659729.html?utm_hp_ref=business&ir=Business.

Powell, C., *CEO on A Mission to Spread Mindfulness*: http://www.ohio.com/business/ceo-on-a-mission-to-spread-mindfulness-1.509673.

Singer, J., *OCD and Mindfulness*: http://psychcentral.com/lib/ocd-and-mindfulness/00020097

Sujato, Bh., *A Brief History of Mindfulness*: http://sujato.wordpress.com/2011/01/18/a-brief-history-of-mindfulness/

Young, S., Five Ways to Know Yourself: An Introduction to Basic Mindfulness: http://www.shinzen.org/RetreatReading/FiveWays.pdf

STOIC MINDFULNESS AND BUDDHIST MINDLESSNESS

Aditya Nain

I'd like to share what might be called a difficulty I face in my attempts to cultivate Stoic dispositions, or, more precisely in my case, to live everyday life according to the guidelines offered by Epictetus. Epictetus and Buddhism share a lot in common and since I have some experience with Buddhist meditation and have been familiar with Buddhism (especially of the Vipassana or 'Insight' school) longer than I have with Epictetus, I tend to compare them, often without realising it. As these comparisons continued to crop up every now and then, I also realised some fundamental differences in practice. These differences are as glaring as the similarities. In this piece, I am going to focus on one of these differences.

The difference is as follows. Epictetus asks one always to keep one's mind ready to counter any impressions that may arise. 'To counter' here is key, since it involves a head on collision of the mind with the impression, or thought. In Buddhist practice on the other hand, impressions (if we can use the same concept at all) are never 'countered'. The aim is not to counter one thought ('I have been robbed') with another ('Material possessions are externals and therefore none of my concern'). It is simply to observe the phenomena and ride the wave of sensation until it subsides. For a practitioner, this is an enormous difference that strikes at the heart of Buddhist or Stoic practice and results in practical difficulties. In fact, the difference is so glaring as to seem irreconcilable and is also extremely important because, for a Vipassana practitioner, to counter one impression with another, is an act of suppression that will lead to the emergence of the impression at another point and possibly in another form.

Let me give another example. Both schools accept a real difference between a phenomenon, its subjective experience and judgments arising as a result of it. They part ways when it comes to dealing with, for example, pain. Epictetus asks you to keep handy a reflection that would immediately counter the "experience-as-pain", for instance that: 'pain belongs to the body and the body is an external'. On the other hand, Buddhist Vipassana asks you not to form a judgment *at all*, because that would merely add another 'layer' to the problem. The aim of Buddhist practice is to realise the difference between the "experience" and the "experienceaspain" and, as such, to observe the "experienceaspain" with complete awareness in order to transcend the painaspect of the experience, something which also involves immersing yourself fully in the experience.

The Stoic technique, in contrast, isolates the mind (i.e. judgments / will) from the experience: the mind stands as something separate from the entire experience. The Buddhist technique (after realising the difference between "experience" and "experienceaspain"), aims to divorce the pain-aspect, while yet keeping the unity of the experience as a whole. The Stoic technique realises the same distinction, but aims to cash in on it and draw the mind out further from the experience, as a tool that stands apart from the experience itself, which is only material or external.

With all this in mind, could it be that Buddhist Vipassana, translated these days as 'mindfulness', is more accurately, 'mindlessness'? Whilst could Stoic practice, on the other hand, be truly characterised as 'mindfulness'?

Perhaps this core difference is a result of the dichotomies that the Stoics work with, i.e. mind and body, internal and external. The Buddhists on the other hand, in the effort to keep the unity of the experience, do not make these distinctions and do not look at the individual as a mind-body complex at all. The mind-body complex gives way to the "five skandhas" (form, sensation, perception, mental formations and consciousness), each of which is integral to the completion of the entire picture of the individual. Materiality is thus not entirely separate from mentality, body does not exclude mind. The internal versus external division is thus not useful within the Buddhist technique.

I do not see a theoretical resolution to what I have tried to describe above. The resolution, if possible, will have to emerge out of practice. It may just turn out that the capabilities achieved through rigorous practice of each are the same. In that case, the theoretical frameworks could remain as they are. However, could one practice both techniques independently and benefit from them? Absolutely. Would the practice of both at the same time be beneficial as well?

I'm not yet very sure of the answer.

WAS THERE A 'STOIC MINDFULNESS'?

Patrick Ussher

If a practitioner of the Early Stoa had been presented with a Buddhist monk practising mindfulness, or sustained awareness, of the breath, he would no doubt have been highly curious as to what the monk was trying to do and, what exactly the *point* of it all was. 'Excuse me, I'm sure your breathing is all very interesting but what does focussing on it have to do with Virtue exactly?' he might have asked. The answer to that question is, in itself, potentially very interesting. In what ways could Buddhist, or Buddhist-inspired, practice inform the Stoic life and vice versa? As Ben Butina argued earlier in Part VII, mindfulness meditation can be a powerful *enabler* of Stoic virtue. Meanwhile, Aditya Nain, for interesting practical and theoretical reasons, took a more skeptical view.

Aside from questions as to how Stoicism might inform Buddhism and vice versa, it is interesting that practitioners of Stoicism often talk about 'Stoic mindfulness' as if there were a kind of mindfulness that is distinct from the Buddhist or Buddhist-inspired forms of mindfulness which are currently so popular in the West. But what would one mean, exactly, by 'Stoic mindfulness'? The word 'mindfulness' clearly has never been used in relation to Stoicism before, historically speaking, so why now?

Part of the answer, I suspect, is that many practitioners of mindfulness meditation, the ability to cultivate more awareness of the present moment, of thoughts and emotions, come to Stoicism and are struck by a perceived similarity. That similarity is *prosoche*, or 'attention', a word used by Epictetus (see *Discourse* 4.12, 'On Attention'). This perceived similarity has led to introducing 'mindfulness' into the Stoic lexicon. At face value, the Stoic emphasis on 'attention', which we also observe in Marcus Aurelius's *Meditations*, might seem rather similar to the idea of 'cultivating awareness' in mindfulness meditation. Indeed, reading through the Stoics can give ample examples of how mindfulness meditation and Stoicism seem to be on the same wavelength. I'll give two such examples, before turning to consider how similar mindfulness meditation and prosoche actually are.

The first is that both 'mindfulness' and 'Stoic mindfulness' emphasize focussing on the present moment. As Marcus Aurelius reminds himself that 'each man lives only in this present moment...all the rest either has been lived or remains in uncertainty' (*Meditations* 10.3) so too does Thich Nhat Hanh, a prominent Buddhist teacher today, say that one ought 'to be aware that we are here and now, and the only moment to be alive is the present moment'. For Thich Nhat Hanh, and other practitioners of mindfulness meditation, to live fully in the present moment is a key source of happiness which stems from the ability to get back 'in touch' with the simpler things in life.

The second key similarity is that both mindfulness and Stoic prosoche prize highly developing *attention* and living a less 'mindless' life. Epictetus considered prosoche to be so essential that he said: 'Do you not realize that when once you have let your mind go wandering, it is no longer in your power to recall it, to bring it back to what is right, to self-respect, to moderation?' (*Discourses*, 4.12). Similarly, Thich Nhat Hanh writes that each action must be done with mindfulness, saying that: 'Each act is a rite, a ceremony...Does the word "rite" seem too solemn? I use that word in order to jolt you into the realization of the life-and-death matter of awareness' (24, 1975).

At this level, something similar seems to be going on, although this is misleading. For these similarities are highly general, and I mention them only so as to show how one *might* think that Stoic prosoche and mindfulness are trying to do the same thing. But, taken at the level above, both Stoic prosoche and mindfulness meditation would also seem similar to, say, the Christian concept of 'wakefulness', as found in the Desert Fathers, early Christian monastics whose teachings are recorded in the *Philokalia*. But one could hardly say that the concerns of the contemporary mindfulness meditator and those of the Desert Fathers are the *same* or, at least they are not usually the same. Indeed, the language of 'paying attention' might be similar, but the overall aims and ends are, of course, very different. (I should note too that there is by no means agreement that the kind of 'mindfulness' practised in a Buddhist context is similar, or indeed anything like, the kind of mindfulness which has been 'adapted' from Buddhism, but then again, nothing is straightforward! See, for example, Dreyfus in Williams & Kabat-Zinn, 2013).

The task at hand, therefore, is to work out what 'Stoic mindfulness' would mean in a Stoic context, with Stoic aims and means. For I do think that it is helpful to call prosoche 'Stoic mindfulness', as it *is* a discipline of paying a kind of attention. But the question is: what *kind* of attention?

Towards an Understanding of 'Stoic Mindfulness'

Prosoche, unlike contemporary mindfulness meditation, is not, in and of itself, concerned with the present moment for its own sake. Rather, it is concerned with applying *key ethical precepts* to how one is living in the present moment.

Epictetus, in *Discourses* 4.12, says that there are two kinds of ethical precept the Stoic practitioner should take with him throughout the day, keeping them attentively (i.e., with prosoche) in mind. They are that 'we must pursue nothing that is outside us, nothing that is not our own, pursue only what is within our will' and, secondly, that 'we must remember who we are, and by what name we are called, and must try to direct our acts to fit each situation and its possibilities.' The first of these refers to Epictetus's standard exhortation that we should focus on 'what is up to us', that is to say, on acting well in our own 'field of agency'. (Importantly, this distinction between what is 'up to us' and 'not up to us' is not just about 'control', as is often thought. Stoicism would not have got very far as a philosophy if it were just about staying calm when your train was late, or if your chariot had broken down: for knowing what 'is up to you' is actually also about what is *ethically* speaking 'up to you'.) The second, which also relates to 'what is up to us', concerns fulfilling our natural and acquired roles well, for example that of father, brother, sister and whatever profession we find ourselves in. This second precept is connected with the idea that real human happiness comes from fulfilling our inherently social nature [*See also Patrick Ussher on 'The Stoics on the Community of Humankind' in Part I*].

So what are the key overarching ideas that a Stoic would keep in mind, or keep 'before him' (with prosoche) in following these two precepts?

On the first precept, the most important thing to keep in mind is the question: 'what is up to me in this situation?' This is largely about working out whether you are valuing the internal or external aspects of a situation more. Put another way, can you value most of all the maintaining or cultivation of your own strength of character and ability to respond well to events, and see this as the principal source of purpose and meaning in the situation? Or do you instead *need* external things, things which are not 'up to you', to be a *certain way* in order to be happy? In adopting the first approach, the situation itself does not change, only your relationship to it does.

On the second precept, the most important thing is to see your relationships as a source of meaning, purpose and happiness and that this can most likely come to fruition by asking oneself questions like: 'How would a good friend respond to this?', 'What are the key points that make up a good teacher?', or 'How can I be a good son in this situation?' The answers to these questions form a kind of ethics which inform, in turn, what is 'up to me'.

Marcus Aurelius provides us with a key example of what applying both of these elements in practice looks like. He writes:

'Every hour focus your mind attentively…on the performance of the task in hand, with dignity, human sympathy, benevolence and freedom, and leave aside all other thoughts. You will achieve this, if you perform each action as if it were your last…' *Meditations*, 2.5

This is Stoic *prosoche* at its clearest: the application of core ethical qualities, as appropriate to the demands of the moment. Marcus's strong ethical sense that what is 'up to him' is to focus *on the craft of the task in front of him* (precept one) but also, in doing this task, to be a kind, benevolent person (precept two). He values most of all the internal: *his own character and how he goes about things*. He does not need 'externals' to be a certain way in order to find happiness or meaning. But we can also see that Marcus's focus on the present moment is not because he thinks the present moment is the source, *in and of itself*, of happiness, as in mindfulness meditation today. Indeed, he is not concerned with developing a moment-by-moment, sensory attention of his present moment experience at all, but with making good ethical use of the present. And that is the key difference between Stoic mindfulness and mindfulness meditation. Whereas the latter is about increasing one's awareness of various aspects of one's experience in the present moment, whether of thoughts, emotions, sensations or 'the moment' itself, Stoic mindfulness is concerned instead with valuing, most of all, responding to the demands of the moment with the qualities it requires: integrity, kindness, humility, courage, or some other kind of quality.

In conclusion, although it is not strictly accurate to call prosoche 'Stoic 'mindfulness', historically speaking, it is probably a helpful term to use as prosoche, like mindfulness meditation, clearly does involve developing a kind of *attention*: Stoic mindfulness is about bringing the two-fold distinction discussed above with you, in the various situations in which you find yourself, *throughout the day*. That's not to say that mindfulness meditation and Stoicism might not inform each other, and to good effect: I've no doubt that they can and do. But it is also important to remember that Stoic prosoche was itself concerned with something very different. It was about being aware of how to act *well* or *ethically* in the present, and not so much about the primacy of the experience of the present itself.

In fact, all Stoic 'mindfulness', or prosoche, is really about is remembering the key precepts of Stoic ethics and putting them into practice.

References:

Dreyfus, G., 'Is Mindfulness Present-Centred and Non-Judgemental? A Discussion of the Cognitive Dimensions of Mindfulness', in Williams M., Kabat-Zinn J. (eds.), *Mindfulness: Diverse Perspectives on its Meaning, Origins and Applications*. Routledge, 2013.
Nhat Hanh, T., *The Miracle of Mindfulness*. Beacon Press, 1975.

PART EIGHT: STOIC LITERATURE AND STOICISM IN MODERN CULTURE

THE EPICTETUS CLUB: STOICISM IN PRISON

Jeff Traylor

Introduction: Of the *Epictetus Club*, Jeff Traylor writes that is a work "...inspired by real events and real people. It is set in the old Ohio Penitentiary. The book follows a group of inmates who meet weekly to study the teachings of the ancient Greek philosopher Epictetus, a former slave and prisoner who used adversity to become wiser and more compassionate. The group is led by an unforgettable lifer named Zeno, a former professional boxer who points out that our greatest opponent is our own thinking. Zeno compares thinking skills to boxing skills, and teaches the men the ABC's of Inner Boxing and the Ten Rounds to Self-Mastery. The reader sits in on life-changing group sessions where the men discuss finding a sense of purpose, "knocking out" excuses, turning adversity to benefit, converting entitlement to gratitude, identifying consequences of actions and how others are affected, handling provocation, dealing with stress, and many other key life lessons.

The descriptions of the institution are factual. Some events described as having taken place at the Ohio Penitentiary actually took place at Marion Correctional Institution. The inmate characters are fictional composites, and the names of staff have been changed. My primary purpose when I began this book was to provide a refresher for the men who had completed a course in cognitive skills that I teach in a community-based correctional facility. By the time the men finish the course, they have studied many of these ideas, and this book is a practical and informative way for them to review the lessons as they prepare to return to society. As the writing progressed, a second use for the book evolved – to provide these concepts and ideas to probationers or inmates at other correctional facilities who do not have access to these kinds of groups."

The book starts with 'The Epictetus Rap':

'My name is Epictetus, here's what I'm puttin' down,
 If you ain't got your cog skills, you're nothin' but a clown.
You know I was a prisoner, you know I was a slave,
It took all of my mind to control how I behave.
But I used my brain to live, I used my brain to get through,
I let go of entitlement, thinking I was due
Whatever I wanted, whatever anyone had,
I learned to focus elsewhere, then I didn't feel so bad
 I took my better feelings and opened up my mind,
I saw I used closed thinking, I saw that I was blind
To all my choices, all my options, all my possibility
And I made a vow right then that I knew I could be free
In my mind and in my heart
And in my thoughts is where to start.
So let me tell you what to do if you truly want to live
A life you can be proud of, a life where you can give
Instead of taking all the time,
 doing booze and drugs and crime.

Clear your head, clear your conscience,

Clear your record, clear your mind,

Ain't no satisfaction in immediate grati-faction.

Now I know you think your circumstance

Is the reason for your victimstance,

But you know it ain't like that

You can survive like a cat.

Turn it on its ear, turn it upside down,

Instead of being crushed, ask how you can turn it 'round.

Don't just do the time, don't be a stupid fool,

This here is a place where if you play it cool,

You'll be stronger in your thinking, stronger in your heart,

When you come up out of here,

You'll now know where to start

 To live a life of purpose, to live the life you need,

To let go of your past, your demands and your greed.

Instead of robbin' in the hood, but sayin' you are good,

Get yourself on home, forget that Robin Hood syndrome.

Don't be makin' no excuses, don't be blamin' no one else,

Take responsibility and be Master of Yourself.'

The Epictetus Club: Extract

At seven sharp the meeting began. Zeno again welcomed all of us and gave a quick review of our last meeting. "Who remembers what 'F.A.I.L.' means?" he asked.

Eddie spoke up. "Fear, Apathy, Inertia, Lack of Vision. These are the four walls that keep us in the box."

"Right. Tonight we're going to talk about getting past these walls – or to use Animal's terms, to leave the well and go to the ocean. And we'll start with a campfire by the water. I'm going to paint two scenarios for you and I would like for you to choose the one you would prefer. In the first scenario, you are walking by the campfire and you trip and fall and your hand goes into the fire. In the second scenario, you are walking by the campfire, you trip and fall, and your head hits a rock and knocks you out as your hand goes in the fire. Which of these two would you prefer?"

The men looked puzzled for a moment, then one of them said, "The first one."

"Why?" asked Zeno.

"Because I could pull my hand out right away." Some of the others nodded in agreement.

Another man said that he would prefer the second scenario, saying that this was "...because I wouldn't feel the pain if I was knocked out." A few others shared his opinion.

The first man then said, "Just because you don't feel the pain doesn't mean that damage isn't being done. What will happen to your hand if you don't pull it out of the fire?"

The second man then admitted that it would probably burn off, and he asked if he could change his answer to the first scenario.

"Pain and consequences have a good purpose," explained Zeno, "but only if we pay attention to them. They can motivate us to make changes, to pull our hand out of the fire, but only if we are aware of them. Consequences without awareness are ineffective." By now everyone was agreeing that the first scenario would be the better choice – that it would be better to feel the pain for a moment to avoid long term damage.

"All of us in here have probably had our hand in the fire for some time, but we have ways of playing it off, making it seem like no big deal," he said as he pulled his right hand up into his sleeve to the laughs of the men. "How do we keep ourselves unconscious to the negative consequences and pain we have brought into our lives?"

"By doing drugs and alcohol," answered Shakes. "That is what I did, and I woke up in here – with a ten year headache!"

"Hanging out with my friends who are into the same stuff as me – they all have just one hand, too, so it looks normal to us," offered another.

"I hang out with people who have no hands – that way I look really good while I'm burning up," added a third man.

"Just telling myself it's not so bad, even though it is," said another.

"Not thinking about it at all."

"Being the life of the party is how I did it," said Animal.

"You guys get the idea," said Zeno. "We have ways to block out the pain and consequences in our lives, and to even make ourselves look good while we do it, but we still get the negative results, no matter what. Since we all agreed that it is better to pull our hand out of the fire as soon as possible, let's do a little activity to increase our awareness of the consequences. This is not to show us how bad we are, but to show us how bad of a life we are creating and to motivate us to make changes – to save ourselves and our families from further damage."

He then introduced the next activity by quoting Epictetus: "Determine what happens first, consider what that leads to, and then act in accordance with what you've learned."

Zeno asked the men to consider some of the results they had received from living a criminal lifestyle, and they went around the circle taking turns as Zeno listed their answers on the board. Loss of freedom, stress, anger, debts, loss of respect from family, loss of self-respect, bad role model for their kids, loss of job, depression, health problems, anxiety and looking over your shoulder all the time were the first round answers. The board filled up after a couple more rounds of answers, and Zeno then broke the list into categories: physical, emotional, social, mental, financial, spiritual, and he added one more category – others. "Who else pays these prices right along with us?" he asked.

171

"My kids," answered Shakes immediately.

"My employer lost a lot behind this," said Leonard. "By the time he found and trained someone to take my place, he almost went under. And that would have cost his other workers their jobs, too."

"The taxpayers also lose," said Animal.

"I don't agree with that," said another. "I've been paying taxes all my life, so this is just getting my own money back."

"Are you saying that instead of your taxes going to roads, schools, and hospitals, they were going for your future stay in prison?" replied Animal. "Instead of an Individual Retirement Account, you set up an Individual Incarceration Account? I can just see the banker's face on that one!"

The group cracked up, with the first man finally agreeing that the taxpayers did, in fact, pay for his room and board at the Walls. Some of the other answers Zeno listed on the board included victims and their families, parents, aunts, uncles, nieces and nephews, society, and friends.

"Now please take out a piece of paper and draw a circle in the middle of it about the size of a quarter. In the circle write the words 'old life'. This represents the old life that you were living that led to your coming to prison. Draw four short stems off of that circle and put a circle at the end of each of those stems. In each of these four circles write one price that you are paying or have paid for that life. Think of a price from several of the categories, but one of your circles must include the word 'others.'"

After a couple of minutes the men had completed filling in the circles. Zeno then instructed them to draw three stems off each of the four circles and write in a price in each circle that was the result of the earlier circle. "For example, if you listed stress in one of your circles, ask yourself 'what does this lead to?' Maybe it leads to anger, which you would put in one of the three circles off of stress. Maybe it causes fights with your wife or girlfriend. Or maybe when you're stressed you get headaches. With each circle ask yourself, 'what does this lead to?' and then write it in a circle. Off of the 'others' circle draw three circles and put the names of three people who are paying these prices along with you, and then from those circles follow it out with how they are paying and what that leads to for them."

After another minute or so Zeno said, "I'm going to give you some time to keep doing this. Keep drawing new stems and circles off of each previous circle and put in a price that is caused by the preceding circle. And while it may not seem like it, the more circles you can come up with, the better."

The men were completely absorbed in the task until Zeno eventually stopped them and asked them to look at their diagrams and make any observations they could about the circles.

"I can't believe how much trouble can come from just one thing!"

"It's all negative."

"I keep seeing the same things popping up in more than one circle."

"How many of you noticed the same old thing repeating itself?" asked Zeno.

All hands went up. "It's like a dog chasing its tail around in a circle," noted Eddie. "All mine eventually lead to anger, jail, drugs, or death, no matter which of the four circles I started with."

"I never realized how many other people were hurt by my actions. I just never thought about it before, and I can't believe what I see here – but I have to believe it, cause it's right here in front of me!" said another. "Selling drugs leads to getting arrested that leads to being away from my kids that leads to them having problems in school that leads to my oldest boy quitting school that leads to him having a lot of problems with employment and finances. It's almost overwhelming for me to see this. This can affect my future grand-kids – and I thought I was doing something to help my family!"

Everyone sat quietly for a few minutes looking at the results of their old life on the papers they held in their hands.

Another group member who had not spoken at the previous meeting finally broke the silence. "Our traditions teach that one should consider the effects of his actions on the next seven generations," offered Manny, a Native American about thirty years old with coal black hair and deep-set eyes. He was studying the traditional teachings of his people and was challenging the rule in court that all inmates must wear short hair. "If you can say that your actions will not harm your descendants, then you may go ahead and act."

"That is certainly taking a long view outside the box, Manny," said Zeno. "Thank you for sharing the ancient wisdom from your culture. It's interesting to see how similar some of these old teachings are. If I may go back to our campfire example for a minute, by doing the circle exercise we are now more likely to pull our hands out of the fire before we burn them off because we are now conscious of the pain. What you have done here is not give yourself any more negative consequences than you had before – you just increased your awareness of the prices you and others are already paying or will likely pay in the future. And who knows – it may very well affect the next seven generations, like Manny said."

Zeno drew the nine dots on the board, and then placed just one circle in the nine dots. "Not thinking about what leads to what keeps us in the box." He then drew the stems and circles off of the first circle so they fell outside the box, and said, "All of these prices you identified beyond the first circle represent an increased awareness, or thinking outside the box. And thinking outside the box leads to a life outside the box.

"This circle exercise is a mental tool that we can use to move beyond the F.A.I.L. (*Fear, Apathy, Inertia, Lack of Vision*) barriers that keep us in the box. The first of these barriers is fear. When you think about actually changing, what are some fears that come up?"

"I'm afraid that I would lose my friends if I changed my ways," said one man.

"I'm afraid I'd have a boring life."

"I'd miss the fast and easy money," said another to the nods of several group members.

174

"I'm afraid I'd fail and just fall back into my old ways."

"I'm afraid of the temptations."

"I'd lose the respect of my associates if I changed."

Zeno listed these fears on the board, and then asked each man to write his fear on a piece of paper. "Now hold your paper with the fear on it at arm's length in your left hand and your circle page at arm's length in your right hand. That is the trade you are making – you are paying all of those prices in your right hand to not face the fear in your left hand."

He then turned to the man who feared losing his friends and asked him if his friends were worth all the prices in his circles, which included being alone in the prison and away from his friends. "I can see that my old ways actually caused the very thing I said I feared – I'm more alone now than ever. Plus, there is no way any friends are worth all the prices I'm paying. Hell, I never hear from them anyway now that I'm locked up."

Zeno then asked another man if he enjoyed the repetitive routines and day-to-day sameness of getting up at the same time, marching to the mess hall at the same time, getting counted at the same time, going to the commissary at the same time, and going to bed at the same time.

"Hell, no, you'd have to be crazy to like that!" he answered.

"But that is exactly what you are getting in your effort to not be bored, isn't it?"

"I see what you mean – I'm paying the price of living a boring life so that I don't have to risk living a boring life. It's the dog chasing his tail again, isn't it."

"Before you say anything else, Zeno, I already see what fast and easy money has brought me," said Eddie. "When I look at all the circles in my right hand, that fast and easy money was anything but fast and easy. I would have done much better with a minimum wage job if you count all the time and money it has cost me – not to mention what it has done to my family."

"And my fear of failing brings me circles such as stress, depression, anger, loss of family, debts, lost jobs, and so much more. I can hardly say that all these circles represent a resounding success!" confessed another man.

Zeno then addressed the idea of temptation. "What is it that makes something tempting to us?" asked Zeno.

"Obviously it is something that we want and like," answered the man who had listed a fear of temptations.

"Right. But if you look at the big picture and see where it all leads, you may find it is not as tempting. If you include being locked up, away from your family, and all the other circles on your paper, you'll find that those old temptations are suddenly not as tempting as before. Think big picture, outside the box."

At this point, Animal chimed in, saying that reminded him of a dog story. "If you don't count all of the long term prices in these circles," he said, "it is like trying to just walk the front half of a dog. We all like the front half of the dog – it licks you, you get to feed it, and all that – but we don't want what comes out the back half of the dog – the smelly messy part. But a dog has both ends, and so do our actions. You can't just take the front half of the dog for a walk – like partying or doing crimes – without taking the back half. You have to take the whole dog."

"And a pooper-scooper," added Eddie to the laughter of the others.

"Thanks, Animal – I guess!" said Zeno good-naturedly. He then moved on to the man who listed losing the respect of other inmates. Zeno pointed out that Epictetus saw this as a particularly harmful fear, and quoted from the *Handbook*: "Those who pursue a better life must be prepared to be ridiculed or criticized by their former associates. Many people who have progressively lowered their personal standards in order to win acceptance from others will bitterly resent those who seek to better themselves. Never live your life in reaction to those poor souls. Be compassionate toward them, and at the same time hold to what you know is good. It is your job to carry yourself with quiet dignity and to stick to your ideals and goals. Cling to what you know in your heart is best. If you are steadfast, those very ones who ridiculed you will come to admire you."

After the discussion of how to counter fears with the circle diagram, which he compared to a warrior's shield that can protect us from bad decisions, Zeno moved on to the other walls of the box. "You can also use these circles to counter the next two letters in F.A.I.L. – apathy and inertia," he said. "Motivation is the great counterpunch to fear, apathy and inertia, and if all these prices we are paying don't motivate us to care and make an effort to change, I don't know what will. Epictetus said that a half-hearted spirit has no power and that tentative efforts lead to tentative outcomes. Use these circles to power up your motivation to move out of the well.

"There is one letter left in our four letters of F.A.I.L., and Epictetus thought it was the most important one – lack of vision or purpose. In fact, he said that evil did not exist naturally in the world or in people, but was a byproduct of forgetting our true aim and purpose in life. We are out of time tonight, but next week we'll talk about that one. Have a good week, gentlemen."

And with that the men walked out of the Death House and across the cold, windswept yard to their cells.

Please note: if you would like to have a free PDF copy of The Epictetus Club, *please email the author (epictetusclub@aol.com).*

THE PHOENIX CYCLE: STOIC SCI-FI

Bob Collopy

Introduction: The following is an extract from the upcoming series, *The Phoenix Cycle*, which aims to capture many philosophies and blend them into a single story line. Each philosophy is represented by one of the main characters. Some philosophies (characters) work together whilst other philosophies do everything they can to destroy the others. In this extract, Johnny is actually a Stoic philosopher while 'The General' is the Marquis de Sade.

The General walked over to Johnny and held out a glass for Johnny to take. "Oh, of course!" The General set the wine glasses on the arms of his wooden chair and came back to untie Johnny's arm. Johnny continued to gaze into the fire, hypnotized as the young girl slowly blew away into the setting sky.

"So let me guess," said The General as he began loosening the rope that had curled itself into a tense knot around Johnny's right wrist. "She was the girl next door. You grew up seeing her on the other side of your window…

"Occasionally, you could muster the strength to 'run into' her when you were taking out the trash." The General raised an eyebrow and begrudgingly changed his tone as he continued his hypothesis.

"When you saw she had brought other boys home, you found that time had halted while you laid in your bed…the only sensation you got from your evening dinner was from its steam, which fumigated your face."

The General droned on. "But when the boy had gone you were first in line to offer a shoulder. You became her friend." The General glanced up and cringed. "You were, 'nice.'"

The General returned his attention to the knot. "But somehow, someway, you bridged that friendship gap, didn't you.

"How nice.

"And she was amazing wasn't she. Oh, she wasn't perfect but her imperfections made her all the more real. Which is exactly what you wanted. She had become more than an image on the other side of the window. She became yours."

The knot around Johnny's wrist melted and slid off.

Johnny's arm dropped down and hung motionless, unaroused by its regained freedom. The General looped around Johnny's chair and drew a long rod from his bag. Johnny's eyes began to leak as sorrow flooded his cognizance. The General paced over to the fire, the grass quietly crunching beneath his feet. The flames mirrored themselves upon his night black aviators.

"Someone cared - you were actually worth something. Your actions had meaning. She made you feel like a real man." The General took a long breath and began to stoke the fire with the long metal rod with Johnny sitting just over his back left shoulder.

"She gave you virtue." The metal rod glided over the burning young girl's hand. It slid beneath her fingertips and slowly began to elevate her hand upward.

"Stop!", shouted Johnny.

The General turned towards the trembling young man strapped to the chair. Johnny's heart fell silent. The fire didn't dare crack. The General stared into Johnny's green eyes, his countenance devoid of expression. The poker went still, and held the young girl's hand.

The two stared at one another. Johnny shook uncontrollably as his eyes sunk into the mordant tar pits of The General's glasses. Blackness spilled out from the aviator's reflective lenses, threatening to blot out Johnny's peripherals and choke him in a world of darkness. Sadly, even with a free hand Johnny couldn't get a grip.

The General's face suddenly cringed. He threw the poker upward and stabbed it into the charcoals of the fire. The young girl's hand fell back into the flame. The General went at Johnny and whipped out a pistol from his jacket. The General shoved the gun into Johnny's face. "So, you can talk!" The General grabbed Johnny's shoulders and shook him so violently Johnny's neck felt a quick snap.

"You want me to stop!", shouted the General, his voice trebled like a 40-year smoker. The General pressed his face close to Johnny snapping his jowls like a Rottweiler ready to rip his face off, "You want this to be over!"

The General reared back and grabbed Johnny's forearm. He slapped the pistol into Johnny's hand. "Then end it!" The General jammed the gun into his own chest.

Johnny swooned in his chair, unable to grasp fully The General's suicidal behavior. He felt like he was broiling beside the flames. His lips moved mechanically, as if in some kind of built-in defense mechanism. "I have virtue."

The General cringed, "You! Virtuous?! Dump that half-assed belief that by restraining yourself from doing what you lust for, you are somehow virtuous!"

Johnny looked up into the black clouded sky. "I follow nature's river."

"Follow nature's river?" The General looked up at the same dead sky and began to patronize. "I don't remember the last time water came from those clouds."

"The world began as fire. It will end as fire. It's okay. I will go with nature. I will lose my way to passion."

"Alright, that's enough." The General backhanded Johnny repeatedly.

Johnny fell out of his meditative state. The General shouted, "The only fire you need to worry about is the spark from my shell casing!"

Johnny's eyes fell upon The General's reflection-less aviators.

"Not a slave to passion?" The General shouted. "Nature is passion! Nature doesn't think! It does not reflect, it does not question what it does. It only does what it feels.

"Now do it! Listen to what you want right now and do it! Follow that river, let it run with blood!" The General's thumb crept up to the gun's barrel and cocked back the firing hammer.

"No," mumbled Johnny.

"You think being passive will stop me?" The General looked behind himself and pointed at the fire, "They thought that too!"

Johnny glanced at the stack of burning flesh. He began hyperventilating, his beliefs strained. The gun shook wildly in his hand, fighting with itself on what to do.

The General saw Johnny's finger slowly nearing the hair-pin trigger. The General breathed venom, "I killed the love of your life, I killed everyone you ever knew! I have taken everything, everything away from you!" The General lowered himself to Johnny's quivering eye level and spoke with Romeo-like passion, "...and I loved it."

Johnny tried to push through the burning pain, but couldn't help acknowledging the capabilities of the gun in his hand. The gun's sights drunkenly swayed. The General shook Johnny and barked, "You feel that? That urge secreting from your loins!" The General drove his fist into Johnny's groin. Johnny lurched forward. The General's arm grabbed his hair and pushed him back up. "You feel it don't you! That burning desire...to kill me? You feel it infecting you more with every pump of your heart." The General brought his head back, he let the fire crackle. His head tilted. "It's arousing isn't it?"

Johnny's lips quivered as they parted, "I just want to be happy..." The General crept in, his hand placed itself reassuringly on Johnny's shoulder, the other kept the gun's barrel pointed square at his chest. "Good. Then you know what you have to do, because you and I both know...I'll never stop."

"But I can't...I can't be happy if I am some...some monster. A monster like you!" Johnny pushed himself away from The General's cold embrace. He screamed. His DLS cracked. Johnny swung the gun under his head and pulled the trigger.

Bang.

A quick flash shot out from the barrel. A casing flung out from the chamber and pinged against The General's aviators. Smoke puffed out from the barrel between the slits of the gun and Johnny's chin. Sulfur invaded their lungs.

Johnny looked at The General, wide eyed, in total shock. The General glared at Johnny. He huffed and slowly rolled his head around. Johnny's hand began to quiver again, but continued to jam the gun into the floor of Johnny's chin.

"God, you are stupid," The General said. The General stood up, growling as he did so; his older age keeping him down. He swiped the quivering gun from Johnny's hand. The General stood over Johnny and spat, "You really think you could do that?"

The General pointed the gun at Johnny's chest and fired in three rapid successions. Johnny winced with every shot as his will to live slowly rose to stable levels. The General shook his head as he watched Johnny squirm in his seat.

"Idiot."

The General turned on his heel and walked back to the fire. He grabbed the metal poker and drew it out of the fire. He looked up into the distance and waited for the last ray of light to trickle away.

SOCRATES AMONG THE SARACENS

Jules Evans

It can still feel weird discussing having had depression and anxiety to strangers in public talks. Although I'm fairly used to exposing myself these days (as it were), there are still occasions when I think 'Is this really a good idea?' I had that feeling this week, standing in front of a gym full of colossal rugby players at Saracens rugby club, one of the leading rugby clubs in the U.K., staring at me stony-faced as I discussed how philosophy helped me through panic attacks.

I was invited to Saracens' training ground in St Albans to give a talk about ancient philosophy, virtue ethics, and the Greeks' ideas on the good life. I believe, and Saracens also believe, that ethics are right at the heart of sport. Sportspeople, on a daily basis, are faced with the questions that Socrates first raised: is it worth being an ethical person? What is the appropriate trade-off between external and internal goods? What does it mean to succeed at life? How do we cope with external pressures and still maintain a good character?

We, the spectator-public, like to think that professional sportspeople are shining knights, that sports coaches are founts of moral wisdom like Coach Taylor in Friday Night Lights. While a lot of our society has become instrumentalized by the language of technocratic management, we still use moral discourse when it comes to sport – we talk about a team's 'values', 'character' and 'philosophy'. The word 'stoic' may have more or less disappeared from academic philosophy, but it's still ubiquitous in the sports pages (stony-faced Ivan Lendl is the latest to be awarded the 'stoic' accolade).

Perhaps we have tried to fill the 'god-shaped hole' with sports, to use sportspeople for ethical role-models and matches as an outlet for collective ecstasy.

England, once the country of religious ecstatics like William Blake or John Wesley, now only allows itself to feel ecstasy when watching sports (or dancing at music festivals). We have secularised ecstasy, much as we secularised Blake's hymn, 'Jerusalem', and turned it into a stadium singalong. This sacralization of sport leads to over-the-top gushing like the reaction to Andy Murray's Wimbledon victory, greeted as if Britain had been religiously redeemed by Murray's sacrifice. Consider this paragraph from *The Times*, for example:

'Joy puts it too conservatively. This was beyond all earthly concepts of joy: this was, for a few moments of eternity, nothing less than bliss. This really is something pretty immense: something nobody from this country has done since the world was young, something he has dedicated his life to...by the end it really seemed as if something more than a sporting prize had been won – as if some mythical, mystical quest had been achieved. It didn't feel like a mere metaphor when he at last picked up that magic golden cup; it really seemed that this really was the Holy Grail.'

Well, quite.

Yet while we look to professional sports to fill an ethical, emotional and religious vacuum, it's also big business and a razzle-dazzle spectacle, with huge amounts of money involved and an intense focus on winning at any cost. David Priestly, who is head of the Personal Development Programme at Saracens, says: 'People have an incredibly romantic view of professional sports. But it can be a very brutal world, a machine that squeezes everything out of a person and then tosses them aside. Most of the people in that world are very far from being role-models. Most people in professional sports shy away from anything explicitly about ethics. It's just about winning. Younger players can see people at the top of their sport who are doing very well while still behaving in a questionable manner.'

The Saracens Revolution

Which brings us to Saracens. The club was 50% bought by a South African consortium in 2009, who appointed Edward Griffiths as the CEO – the man who'd managed South African rugby in the run-up to their nation-building 1995 World Cup victory. Griffiths promised a 'Saracens Revolution' which would turn rugby into a glitzy, entertaining and crowd-pleasing spectacle. Saracens matches would alternate between Wembley and a new astroturf stadium in north London, match attendance would rise from 14,000 to 80,000, spectators would be able to watch replays on their smartphones, even order pizzas from their seats. The club was now in the business of 'making memories'.

But the other side of the Saracens Revolution was a focus on character and virtues, as proclaimed by the South African director of rugby, Brendan Venter. He's a doctor, a Christian, and something of a rebel, who's surprised journalists with comments like: 'You can't think about winning all the time. I'm far more interested in my players, along with me, improving as people. That's basically the only thing that really matters.' He's also said: 'If we win everything there is to win but we've broken relationships, we've lost the plot. We've missed our point of being on earth, it's as simple as that.'

Venter, who studied to be a doctor while playing rugby, insisted the players need to be well-rounded and prepared for life after rugby. They need to be cared for as individuals with souls rather than commodities shoveled into the money-furnace. Their academic pursuits should be just as important as their physical fitness. Players were asked to write essays on 'the ideal 20-year-old' and to think about questions like: 'How does the ideal 20-year-old treat women? How does the ideal 20-year-old treat alcohol? How does he handle his finances? How does he deal with life in general?'

Alex Goode, the 25-year-old Saracens and England full-back, saw the revolution first-hand, having come through the Saracens Academy as a teenager. He says: 'The old Saracens was not a particularly friendly place. There'd be quite brutal banter. Players lived spread out across Hertfordshire and hung out separately A lot of the players were in it for their own benefit and not the team, they didn't make sacrifices for the team. Now, there's much more of a feeling of togetherness. The players and families are really taken care of, and the flip-side of that is we have to work incredibly hard.'

The Revolution seems to be succeeding. Having never won the English rugby premiership, Saracens were runners-up in Venter's first season (2009-2010), then won it in 2010-2011. This season, however, has been tough – they led the Premiership by wins and points, but then lost in the play-off semi-final, and also lost in the Heineken Cup semi-final to Toulon. The defeats raise the age-old question again: is it worth putting character before external success?

The Jerry Maguire of Sports Coaching

Venter stepped down as director of rugby and went back to South Africa in 2011, following a series of family bereavements back home, but he's still technical director. The ethical revolution, meanwhile, continues through the Saracens Personal Development Programme, which is run by David Priestly and David Jones. The latter David is a philosophy grad, who read my book and got in touch. He has the unique vision that philosophy has a place in professional sports – and he's stuck his neck out by inviting me to speak to the lads.

His boss, 34-year-old David Priestly, has a remarkable, zen-like calm about him. He is something of a Jerry Maguire-figure in that he genuinely believes winning isn't everything. He says the 'performance-based myopia' of professional sports can be morally corrupting for players and staff. This is somewhat heretical in professional sports, even in the world of 'performance lifestyle coaching', which is meant to provide care and guidance for sportspeople but is often just as obsessed with winning at any cost.

Priestly is different. He's nick-named 'The Priest' at the club because he is something like a moral compass for the team, keeping them honest, challenging them to live by their mission-statement, rather than just hanging it prominently on the wall. What happens, for example, if a match-winning player fails to meet the ethical standards of the club? Will that player be dropped before a big game? Does the club care as much for a third-team player as a first-team star? It's in such line-calls that you see the tension between the Saracens Revolution's two goals of sport-as-character-development versus sport-as-profitable-public-spectacle. Inner goods versus outer goods, in other words.

I get the sense Priestly has made the personal choice to put character before external success. He doesn't seem beholden to conventional success or status, and is not afraid of being sacked. He tells me: 'Players can smell it a mile away when you say one thing but behave differently. But if you genuinely live by what you teach they will respond to that.' He has the backbone to stand by his beliefs even in a high-pressure workplace, and the wisdom to recognise that even hard-as-nails rugby men need the occasional opportunity to be vulnerable.

He has written:

'In my opinion it is neither 'soft' nor 'fluffy' nor easy to listen to someone sharing their innermost difficulties. In fact, when someone feels able to bare their soul and be completely vulnerable in my company, I actually believe it to be an incredibly privileged experience. (Sports psychologists) obsessed with performance will never even get close to touching this kind of information...When you are told that you need to be tough, why show that you are vulnerable?'

He gives me some advice as I go in to talk to the players: 'They will be interested. They might put forward a tough-guy front, but they'll be listening intently.'

Virtue Ethics and Sports Psychology

David Jones tells me he's not sure how many to expect at my talk (this is their first philosopher at Saracens), but there's a good turn-out, 20 or so players and coaches, including various internationals like Chris Ashton and Steve Borthwick. And so, with these assembled tough guys in front of me, I launch into my talk, beginning with how I messed myself up with drugs, got depression and panic attacks, then found help in philosophy. It feels slightly surreal at first, I think to myself 'Am I really doing this? Is this going to work at all?' But I tell myself to keep going.

After the initial weirdness of exposing my soul to a room full of rugby players, I settle into it, confident that virtue ethics has important things to say to sports psychology (and vice versa). Sport is a lot about emotional control, and no one understood emotional control better than the Stoics. They insisted our emotions come from our judgements and perceptions. We can change our emotions by becoming more aware of our beliefs and attitudes, and more skillful in what we say to ourselves.

This is a familiar idea to sports players, who have already been drilled in the importance of 'attitude' to winning, although one of the players asks me if the Stoic idea of controlling your perceptions and emotions means 'always being positive'. I reply that no, being 'philosophical' is not necessarily the same as never feeling negative emotions. Aristotle thought sometimes anger and grief were appropriate responses to life's tragedies. I say this not realizing that one of the team's core values is 'be relentlessly positive and energized at all times'…which sounds a bit exhausting. Surely it's OK to be frightened, angry, upset or lost sometimes?

The Greeks' techniques for creating ethical habits are also obviously useful to sportspeople, particularly the idea of repeating maxims to yourself over and over. Sportspeople already use 'mantras' and mottos to ingrain attitudes, and Saracens has its mission statement posted on the walls around the gym. I talk about the Greeks' idea that excellence isn't just about how you perform in the classroom (or the rugby pitch) – that it extends out into all your interactions, how you treat your wife, your children, the younger players, the referee, how you cope with setbacks in your life. Everything is training.

I get the sense that the players are particularly interested in Epictetus's idea of focussing on the things you can control in life without freaking out over the things you can't completely control (your reputation, your body, other people, the weather etc). Again, this is not a new idea in sports psychology (or management – it's one of Stephen Covey's *7 Habits*), but it still resonates. We talk about not using externals as an alibi for your own bad behaviour – the referee, for example, your team-mates, your wife, your childhood.

Letting go of the past is such a key skill for sportspeople – whether that past is your childhood, the last match or the last point. Andy Murray said in a recent BBC documentary that one of the main things he's worked on in the last year is not wasting energy thinking about past points during games. Priestly says to me, "So much of what I'm trying to get across comes down to the three words: 'Let it go'."

We also talk about the idea of not caring too much about your status and reputation, not building your house on sand as Jesus put it. Professional sports people have to deal with an incredibly volatile status throughout their life, as Alex Goode tells me: 'It's a big shift from schoolboy rugby to professional sports. Suddenly, you go from the blue-eyed boy of your school team to a situation where no one cares if you've played England Under 18s, and you're on the bench and not playing all the games. That's hard to deal with.'

Then, like Goode, you might get to play for England, another huge step-up in terms of pressure and publicity. He says: 'Suddenly, everyone wants to talk to you about rugby. By the end of last season, for the first time, I didn't want to talk about rugby any more, I needed something separate from it.' Goode was then injured and side-lined, thereby perhaps missing the Lions tour. Injuries can be existential crises for sportspeople, depriving them of the activity by which they define and validate themselves. Alex got through the disappointment of his injury partly by having 'something separate' – he tells me he's found pleasure in reading novels, and is interested in becoming a journalist after rugby.

A lot of the volatility of sportspeople's status comes from the media, which can be a circus mirror, distorting reality into simplistic narratives. In 2006, the 19-year-old Andy Murray was being interviewed with his friend Tim Henman. They were teasing each other about the World Cup and Murray joked he'd support 'anyone but England'. The joke was seized on by a journalist and hung round his neck like an albatross for years. It prompted Tony Parsons to fulminate that the comment was 'the tip of a toxic iceberg of anti-Englishness'. Journalists divide humanity into heroes and villains, and sports stars can be canonized one day, demonized the next. They have to live with that volatility of image, accept that its out of their control, and let it go. Not easy.

Not just means, but ends

So there are many meeting points between sports psychology and virtue ethics. What philosophy brings to the table – why Saracens asked me there – is that philosophy isn't just about techniques for on-the-field success. It's also a way to question what success actually looks like, what end or goal we're using all these techniques for. Is winning your ultimate goal – your God – or is there something higher? It's possible to win a lot of medals and lose at life. It's possible to create a highly profitable entertainment spectacle, like the football Premiership, that is nonetheless a pretty immoral and toxic industry.

I end by talking about the idea of honouring your gifts. We're born with certain gifts, blessed with them, the talents we have done nothing to earn. It's up to us what our relationship to these gifts are, whether we honour them or not. The Stoics talked about every person having their own daemon, their inner God. We can have a bad relationship with our daemon, and it can turn against us and destroy us – think of all those incredibly gifted sportspeople (or artists) who ended up destroyed by their gifts. Or, we can develop a proper, healthy relationship to our gifts, honouring them, dedicating them to something higher. The Greek word for 'flourishing' is *eudaimonia*, which you could very roughly translate as 'having a good relationship with your gifts'.

After the talk, several players came up and shook my hand, which was heart-warming, because I'd wondered how my talk would go down, as a small philosopher in a world of big athletes. David Jones' philosophical gamble seemed to have paid off. I came away having learned something from the team about strength. If even rugby players can learn to take care of themselves and each other, if they can learn to find the right balance between banter and vulnerability, between pressure and acceptance, there's hope for us all.

Editor's Note: Jules Evans subsequently ran a philosophy club at Saracens for the course of the 2013-2014 season, which Saracens coach Paul Gustard said was 'the most popular thing we did this season'. You can read more about the course, which Jules also taught at HMP Low Moss prison, at this link: https://emotions-blog.history.qmul.ac.uk/2014/06/philosophies-for-life-the-results-of-the-pilot/

'I THINK EVERY CHILD SHOULD LEARN STOIC PHILOSOPHY' : A CONVERSATION WITH JOHN LLOYD

Jules Evans

Introduction: Jules Evans interviews John Lloyd, the TV producer behind *Not the Nine O'Clock News*, *Blackadder*, *Spitting Image* and *QI*.

How did you come across Stoic philosophy?

I'd had 10 years of unalloyed success as a TV producer in the 1980s – I'd made three blockbuster telly shows, I'd got married, I had two children, two houses, two cars, one whole wall of my office covered in awards, I had money, I was in decent health. And then on Christmas Eve 1993, I woke up and couldn't see the point of anything. It was like running into a wall. I'd had a couple of really awful betrayals, which seemed to happen to me serially – I'd help people then they'd shit all over me. I went right down the hole, became fantastically depressed, very angry and resentful, and spent a lot of time under my desk crying. I was a commercials director then, very successful. And the worst thing was I couldn't understand why I was so unhappy because I had everything. I had no reason to be depressed.

So how did you cope?

The way I saw it was, I had to turn the same kind of determination and intelligence onto myself that I would normally apply to my programming. I set out quite specifically to look for the meaning of life. I needed to find a better reason to go on living than the usual one, which is 'he who dies with the most toys wins'. That didn't work for me anymore - I'd got the toys and they weren't satisfying to me. Let's see if anyone has any better ideas.

I started reading frantically. I started with physics: I learned about quantum mechanics, and it astonished me. I learned what E=MC2 means for the first time – that matter is equivalent to energy and there's nothing really solid there. Then I read *The Agony and Ecstasy* by Irving Stone, about the life of Michelangelo. And in there it mentions how the Medici wanted to recover the wisdom of the ancients, particularly Pythagoras. I thought "He was the guy who invented the triangle". I discovered he was one of the greatest philosophers in history. I thought: that's it! My God! I've discovered Pythagoras, no one else knows about this. I went to Foyles, to the Classics section, and said, rather smugly, 'Do you have any books on sixth and fifth century BC Athens?', thinking there would hardly be anything, and he pointed, there was a whole wall on those two centuries in Greece. I staggered back, thinking it would take ten lifetimes to read all that, and that it's too late at 42.

But I had a go, and along the way I bumped into various people who helped me. I came across Marcus Aurelius very early on. Some of his sayings were incredibly helpful, like 'Waste no more time arguing what a good man should be – be one' (*Meditations*, 4.17). That hit home. Or 'Consider that everything is opinion, and opinion is in your power. Take away the opinion, and like a mariner, who has doubled the promontory, you will find calm, everything stable, and a waveless bay' (*Meditations*, 12.22). I love Marcus Aurelius – this wonderful man with a terrible life, retiring to his room every night to write in his journal and think how to cope.

What do you find particularly useful in Stoicism?

The basic idea that I find useful in Stoicism is that it's all in your attitude. Shit happens, but what distinguishes those who are coping from those who aren't is how they react. There is no requirement to suffer, it's a self-imposed thing. And I love the idea, particularly in Epictetus, that philosophy is a way of life, something we should all practice.

My daughter, who is seventeen, has just bumped into that – she's doing philosophy A-Level. She's fascinated by what Epictetus said about philosophy being a way of life and a love of wisdom. It's not just theoretical, though unfortunately that's how it's usually taught. Academic philosophers are not necessarily wise people. You shouldn't study Heidegger or Nietzsche or Spinoza just to know what they thought, you should see if you can live by it.

My view is every child should study quantum physics and Stoic philosophy. They should learn, 'What do I do when somebody makes me unhappy? Why are people greedy and nasty? What is fear? What should I do when things go wrong?' It staggers me that we don't learn these things at school. In Stoicism, we have this very simple and powerful idea – it's not what happens to you but how you react. That's why I like Stoicism - because it's simple, plain and logical, it doesn't involve any Gods or outside help, it's all in you.

Do you believe in God?

I'm 'ignostic'. I like the definition of ignostic as 'someone who refuses to discuss whether God exists until the terms are defined'. You tell me what you mean by God and then I'll tell you if I believe in it. No one seriously believes in the giant guy with a white beard and sandals. No one thinks that, no one ever has. Even Michelangelo didn't. You're a fool if you think you have any idea what's going on, or if you think anyone does. No one knows why the universe began or even how: the Big Bang Theory is falling to pieces according to Martin Rees [*the astronomer royal*].

I call it "The Great Whatever It Is". I see the universe as conscious and benevolent. I see life as an examination we didn't apply to take, but we're in one, and we have to work out what the rules are and what it means to pass that test. And in that test, we come across those Stoic virtues of self-control and self-knowledge, understanding that most of the bad things that happen to you are self-generated. Resentment, fear, anger, laziness, are all self inflicted – you can decide not to be like that. There's only one task in life, and that is to get a grip on yourself.

How have you combined Stoicism with other philosophies?

My philosophy is unashamedly pick and mix. I had this peripatetic and bizarre route around all the philosophies of the world – the *Tao Te Ching*, the *Bhagavad Gita*, the *Koran, St Augustine, St John of the Cross*, Sufism. I say I'm a Stoic because it's less frightening to people, and less specifically theistic. I think there's only one philosophy, really. One of my favourite books is Aldous Huxley's *Perennial Philosophy* – underneath all the claptrap of religious differences, it's the same thing: my job is to fix me, to quiet my interior rantings, and be nice to everybody else. It works for me. It's a lot less painful trying to be as cheerful and friendly and unjudgmental as you can. It's an effective way of getting by.

Did ancient philosophy get you out of that emotional pit?

I was pretty depressed, but I can say that depression at root is a philosophical problem. It's bound to occur to intelligent people sometimes, especially when things go wrong. You feel the universe is very unfair, but it's not unfair, it's just what is. But the two things that initially helped me most were, firstly, going for very long walks; and secondly, being interested in things, which is where *QI* came from.

STOICISM AND STAR TREK

Jen Farren

The original Star Trek of 1966 was a TV show with big philosophical ideas. The show's creator, Gene Roddenberry, was a humanist who wanted to show characters co-operating with reason and humanity. The show explored ethics, philosophy and politics, had a multi-racial cast and the first televised inter-racial kiss.

But the show also had its own take on Stoicism. Indeed, Gene Roddenberry said that he intentionally created a Stoic character, 'Spock,' as one of the three main characters alongside Dr McCoy and Kirk.

For us fans of Stoicism and (perhaps) of Star Trek, this raises an interesting question: how 'Stoic' is Spock exactly? Is he your genuine 'Stoic sage' or is he more of a 'stereotypical stoic', ignoring emotions and governed purely by reason?

In this article, I set out to find the answer, by exploring the philosophical underpinnings of Star Trek.

Spock: Stereotypical 'stoic' or 'Stoic' sage?

Before we consider this question, let's first look at what makes the ideal Stoic, in the words of Seneca:

'The pilot's art is never made worse by the storm nor the application of his art either. The pilot has promised you not a prosperous voyage, but a serviceable performance of his task - that is, an expert knowledge of steering a ship. And the more he is hampered by the stress of fortune, so much the more does his knowledge become apparent. The storm does not interfere with the pilot's work, but only with his success. "What then," you say, "is not a pilot harmed by any circumstance which does not permit him to make port, frustrates all his efforts, and either carries him out to sea, or holds the ship in irons, or strips her masts?" It is indeed so far from hindering the pilot's art that it even exhibits the art; for anyone, in the words of the proverb, is a pilot on a calm sea...But the wise man is always in action, greatest in performance at the very time when fortune has blocked his way. For then he is actually engaged in the business of wisdom.' *Moral Letters*, 85.

To summarize, the ideal Stoic must show resilience in crisis, know what he can and can't control and *show this by action*. As Seneca writes elsewhere: 'No fortune, no external circumstance can shut off the wise man from action.' So which of the main characters in Star Trek can live up to this ideal?

On the face of it, there are two ways in which Spock might seem a genuine Stoic.

Firstly, he accepts reality, noting if something is in his control or not. He says: 'What is necessary is never unwise.' The Stoic belief is that if we fight what is necessary we will suffer conflict, whilst if we accept it, we can remain calm. Logic like this can simplify life greatly. Marcus Aurelius noted that much of what we say and do is unnecessary. Indeed, he often asked himself: 'Is this one of the necessary things?'

Secondly, Spock observes without adding extra opinion: 'Fascinating is a word I use for the unexpected.' To follow the Stoic rule to only judge things in your control as good or bad, and all else as "fascinating" brings mental calm. It links with the Stoic idea that it is our judgements that upset us more than events. This is about simply stating facts and removing the opinion associated with them.

But both of these aspects are misleading and actually belie Spock's ruthlessly logical character, something which pushes him towards being a small 's', stereotypical 'stoic.'

This is clear in his concern with emotional control: 'Our principles of logic offer a serenity that humans rarely experience in full. We have emotions. But we deal firmly with them and do not let them control us.' This isn't easy for Spock at all. In the episode "The Crying Time", for example, Spock is seen repeating 'I'm in control of my emotions', before bursting into tears. Most crucially of all though, from the point of view of the ideal Stoic being a *man of action*, Spock's over-reliance on logic sometimes leads him to a kind of 'logic-induced' paralysis. He says: 'I have insufficient information' and 'insufficient facts always invite danger.' Therefore, logic tells him the least risk is best or that more facts will create better decisions, but this is a cognitive distortion as modern science tells us there is often no correlation between more information and accuracy. Indeed, Spock's logic makes him defeatist when there is no identifiable logical option or chance of success: 'In chess, when one is outmatched, the game is over, checkmate.' For Spock, logic, and nothing else, is the most important thing.

All in all, Spock is hardly the Stoic sage. Although he has some Stoic leanings, he consistently falls short of being the man of action. Furthermore, in completely suppressing his emotions, he conforms to the stereotype of the Stoic, in contrast to the real Stoic who aims to cultivate positive emotions such as joy and wishing others well.

So if Spock is not your genuine Stoic, then what about McCoy?

McCoy is the polar opposite of Spock: emotion without reason, and as such he is even further away from the Stoic sage. He takes risks which put himself and others in danger. McCoy and Spock are at a stalemate and it's no surprise that most episodes find Spock and McCoy arguing - should reason or emotion be their guide? Consider this exchange:

McCoy: 'I'm sick and tired of your logic.'

Spock: 'That is most illogical, it is more rational to sacrifice one life than six. The needs of the many outweigh the needs of the few or the one.'

Interestingly, this dichotomy is echoed in modern neuroscience. Daniel Kahneman in *Thinking Fast and Slow* says the brain makes use of two systems: System 1 makes rapid decisions based on emotion, while System 2 makes complex decisions based on analysis and logic. Nevertheless, both systems can deliver the Stoic goal of acting for the common welfare. System 1 (McCoy) does this by automatic emotional responses that trigger actions to protect those in danger. He will risk his life for what he *feels* is right. System 2 (Spock) does this by deliberate analysis. He will risk his life if it is *logical*. To him it is illogical to kill without reason, but sometimes it is logical to kill - as such he is ready to sacrifice his life to protect the crew. This dichotomy is echoed in Koenig's study of moral dilemmas about hypothetically harming one person to save many more. Three groups were tested, one of which had impaired emotional function. It found removing the conflict of emotion and reason saved more people as 40% of the group with impaired emotional function agreed to harm one person to save many compared to only 20% in the others.

But what about the last of the trio, Kirk? Is he in any way closer to the Stoic ideal? Kirk says that he doesn't play chess - he plays poker: a game of great skill and risk, all about playing the cards which have been dealt well. Similarly, Epictetus talks about the 'roll of life's dice', and making *careful use* of the dice that has been thrown: 'Imitate those who play dice. Counters and dice are indifferent: how do I know what is going to turn up? My business is to use what does turn up with diligence and skill' (*Discourses* 2.5).

In this way, Kirk tries to balance emotion and reason, but he never loses sight of taking action. His choices and actions make him take risks for the common welfare, even when the purely logical thing might be to do nothing. Perhaps he, as the perfect mixture of good emotions and ethical imperatives, a mixture, as it were, of the best of Spock and McCoy, is Star Trek's real Stoic: *the man of both action and contemplation.* In the words of Captain Kirk himself: 'Gentlemen, we're debating in a vacuum, let's go get some answers.'

But, of course, from the point of view of good cinema, it doesn't matter that the real Stoic in Star Trek wasn't the 'stoic' character. For that Spock should have been portrayed in such a way at all was actually crucial for the dynamics between the main characters in the show. Indeed, each episode explores the conflict of reason and emotion through Spock's relationships with the other characters. Gene Roddenberry (in Edward Gross, 1995) says that he deliberately:

'Took the perfect person and divided him into three, the administrative cou-rageous part in the Captain (Kirk), the logical part in the Science Officer (Spock) and the humanist part in the Doctor (McCoy).'

It is in Star Trek, then, that this perennial source of inner conflict between reason and emotion plays out so clearly. Stephen Fry captures per-fectly how Star Trek dramatized this clash of reason and emotion:

'You have the Captain in the middle, who is trying to balance both his humanity and his reason. And on his left shoulder, you have the appetitive, physical Dr McCoy. And on his right shoulder you have Spock, who is all reason. And they are both flawed, because they don't balance the two, and they're at war with each other, McCoy is always having a go at Spock. And Kirk is in the middle, representing the perfect solution. And not only that, the planets they visit usually make the mistake of being either over-ordered and over-reasonable and over-logical (so they kill those who dissent, and they do it calmly and reasonably), and they have to learn to be a bit human. Or, they are just a savage race that needs reason and order.'

And if Spock had to be made the 'stereotypical Stoic', rather than the

Stoic sage, to bring that perennial human conflict to the big screen sage, then so much the better for generations of Star Trek fans.

References

Central Intelligence Agency. 'Do you really need more intelligence?': https://www.cia.gov/library/center-for-the-study-of-intelligence/csi-publications/books-and-monographs/psychology-of-intelligence-analysis/art8.html

Fry, S., 'How Star Trek Ties into Nietzsche and Ancient Greece': http://trekmovie.com/2011/07/04/video-of-the-day-stephen-fry-explains-how-star-trek-ties-into-nietzsche-and-ancient-greece/

Gross, E., *Captains' Logs: The Unauthorized Complete Trek Voyages*. Little Brown & Co., 1995.

Kahneman D., *Thinking Fast and Slow*. Penguin, 2011.

Koenigs, Young et al., "Damage to the prefrontal cortex increases utilitarian moral judgement", in *Nature*, 446, pp. 908-911, 2007.

86898653R00112

Made in the USA
Lexington, KY
17 April 2018